P9-DMX-859

# The
# Golden
# Retriever

## Handbook

### D. Caroline Coile

**With Full-color Photographs**
**Drawings by Michele Earle-Bridges**

**BARRON'S**

## Acknowledgments

The American breed standard is reprinted courtesy of the American Kennel Club.

The British breed standard is reprinted courtesy of the Kennel Club.

The author is grateful to Alice Woodyard and to Frank Andrews for their suggestions.

© Copyright 2000 by D. Caroline Coile

All rights reserved.

No part of this book may be reproduced in any form, by photostat, microfilm, xerography, or any other means, or incorporated into any information retrieval system, electronic or mechanical, without the written permission of the copyright owner.

*All inquiries should be addressed to:*
Barron's Educational Series, Inc.
250 Wireless Boulevard
Hauppauge, New York 11788
**http://www.barronseduc.com**

ISBN-13: 978-0-7641-1237-9
ISBN-10: 0-7641-1237-6

*Library of Congress Catalog Card No. 99-55650*

## Library of Congress Cataloging-in-Publication Data

Coile, D. Caroline.
     The golden retriever handbook / D. Caroline Coile;
    illustrations by Michele Earle-Bridges.
     p.   cm.
     Includes bibliographical references (p.   ).
     ISBN 0-7641-1237-6
     1. Golden retriever. I. Title.
SF429.G63 C65   2000
636.752'7—dc21                99-55650
                                CIP

Printed in China

19 18 17 16 15 14 13 12

## About the Author

D. Caroline Coile has written many books and articles about dogs for both the scientific and lay press. Among her books are *Barron's Encyclopedia of Dog Breeds* and *Show Me! A Dog Showing Primer*, as well as 13 breed books. Among her dog writing awards are the Denlinger, Maxwell, and Eukanuba Canine Health Awards. She holds a doctorate in the field of neuroscience and behavior, with special interests in canine sensory systems, genetics, and behavior. Her "Baha" Salukis have been top-ranked in conformation, field, and obedience competition with Pedigree Award, Best in Show, Best in Specialty, and Best in Field awards to their credit.

## Photo Credits

Kent and Donna Dannen: pages vi, viii, 2, 5, 7, 27, 28, 31, 33, 34, 36, 44, 52, 54, 62, 64, 69, 77, 80, 86, 92, 96, 102, 104, 106, 108, 113, 119, 120, 127, 128, 135, 140, 144, 157, 160, 172, 175, 181, 189, 192, 195; Susan Rezy: pages 6, 14, 19, 74, 82, 115, 179, 184; Bonnie Nance: 8, 10, 48, 50, 94, 133, 166, 168, 186, 188; Tara Darling: pages 16, 24, 78; Sharon Eide: pages 22, 45, 53, 98, 125, 154, 162, 171, 190; Toni Tucker: pages 39, 173; Isabelle Francais: page 41; Judith Strom: pages 66, 110, 112, 130, 145, 151, 164, 182, 185, 194.

## Cover Credits

Isabelle Francais.

## Important Note

This book tells the reader how to buy and care for a Golden Retriever. The author and the publisher consider it important to point out that the advice given in the book is meant primarily for normally developed puppies from a good breeder—that is, dogs of excellent physical health and good character.

Caution is advised in the association of children with dogs, in meeting with other dogs, and in exercising the dog without a leash.

Even well-behaved and carefully supervised dogs sometimes do damage to someone else's property or cause accidents. It is, therefore, in the owner's interest to be adequately insured against such eventualities, and we strongly urge all dog owners to purchase liability policies that cover their dog.

# Contents

# Preface

Golden Retrievers are overachievers. They can do more in one day than most other dogs do in a year. Golden Retrievers are a step up from the average dog, and their people need information that's a step up from standard dog books. *The Golden Retriever Handbook* was written for the Golden owner who is not content with the standard introductory fare in most dog books. It was written for people who want to excel at Golden guardianship to the same degree that their Golden excels at companionship. It was written with the assumption that, even if you are a new dog owner, you expect more in a dog—and in a dog book—than the same old status quo. That means you won't find pages of information here about what to name your dog or even how to housebreak it. There are plenty of other books around that can tell you that. You also won't find pages of pedigrees. Again, plenty of other books are filled with those. You will find, instead, pages of information about the very latest medical findings relating to Golden Retrievers, dealing with sports injuries, training for field work, behavior problems and obedience, competitions, nutrition, and breeding. If you want the latest information on making the best of your life with your Golden, then this book is for you. If you want the status quo, then neither this book, nor the Golden Retriever, is for you.

*Golden of spirit and form...*

# Chapter One
# The Golden Child

The morning silence is broken by a golden shape plunging into icy water; city street sounds mask the steady footsteps of a golden dog in harness guiding his sightless charge; the crowd's applause is kept time by a wagging gold tail as the judge awards High in Trial; laughter breaks through worry as golden jaws attempt to set a new record for the number of tennis balls held; a child's nightmares are soothed by a golden presence…

The Golden Retriever is many dogs to many people, a dog of such varied talents and golden heart that its popularity is no surprise. Perhaps the only surprise is that no such golden souls existed until fairly recently.

## A Dog for Every Job

Since the first domesticated dogs, humans have found that by breeding dogs with desirable traits to one another, the likelihood increased of producing more such dogs. By classical Roman times,

*There was gold in those Scottish hills…*

dog breeding had reached the point that most of the modern families of dogs were firmly established. Retrievers, however, were not among them. The reason was simple: The hallmark ability of the retriever is to bring back birds the hunter can't easily reach. Until the advent of guns, birds were usually caught by falcons or by throwing large nets over them. Only when hunters downed birds with guns were they regularly confronted with the problem of getting the birds, which may have fallen far afield or in deep water.

With the first muzzle-loading firearms, bird dogs that traditionally were used only to find and point out game began also to be trained to retrieve it. The breech-loading shotgun entered the scene in the mid-1800s, raising the requirements for retrieving. Whereas a good day's hunting with a muzzle loader entailed much walking and might have produced ten shot birds, the ease and accuracy of the newer guns made it simpler to shoot birds in flight, making them more likely to fall in inaccessible places and at a distance. Birds were so easily shot that the limiting factor became the numbers of the birds themselves. Wealthy landowners employed gamekeepers to raise and release birds, and beaters drove birds toward stationary hunters. Shooting no longer required great outdoorsmanship, but it still required skill, time, land, and birds—the ideal combination to elevate it to the new fashionable pastime of the rich.

Sometimes, shooting parties were part picnic and part fashion show, and certainly few of the participants were eager to trudge after all the downed birds. As the finer estates tried to outdo each other in terms of house parties, game, and dogs, the pressure was on their kennelmen to perfect a dog that would stay close until the shooting stopped, find the dropped birds, and return them without damage. Around 1840 greater attention began to be aimed at creating a dog that was a specialist retriever. Such a dog would be a good swimmer, very obedient, strong, with a good nose and soft mouth, but with less interest in ranging far afield to hunt on its own.

The existing setters in their kennels were usually interested in picking up birds, but were not always reliable about returning them in good condition, nor were most of them suited for getting birds that had fallen in water. Water spaniels were more adept in water, but the key ingredient came in the form of the "Lesser Newfoundler," a breed developed in Newfoundland as an all-around fisherman's helper. Here was a dog that could carry items in

*The Golden's ability to perform not only as an upland game retriever, but also a natural water retriever, made it an ideal gentleman's hunting companion.*

its mouth through strong seas, at the direction of the fisherman, and some hunters had already discovered that those same qualities made them outstanding water retrievers for birds. The first of these dogs, later to become known as Labrador Retrievers, came to Britain in the early 1800s. Crosses of either Water Spaniels or Setters to smaller varieties of Newfoundlands were proving to produce the best retrievers known to date—but they still weren't Golden Retrievers.

# The Dogs of Lord Tweedmouth

The ingredients were all there. Now all that was needed was a master to combine them, the conditions under which to test them, the resources with which to refine them, and a lot of luck. The master came in the person of Dudley Coutts Marjoribanks (later to be called the first Lord Tweedmouth), a sportsman, dog afficionado, and serious breeder of many fine animals, who owned the Guisachan estate in the Scottish highlands near the Tweed River. Among his dogs were spaniels and retrievers, but the most fateful addition came from a chance encounter with a golden-coated retriever owned by a cobbler. Since the cobbler had no use for him, he sold the dog (named Nous) to Marjoribanks, who in 1868 bred him to one of his Tweed Water Spaniels, Belle. From this union emerged four yellow

GOLD   NUGGET

**The Circus Tale**
A fanciful, but discredited, tale of the Golden's origin maintained that Lord Tweedmouth's dogs descended from a troupe of Russian circus dogs.

retrievers named Crocus, Cowslip, Primrose, and Ada. They were to become the foundation of the Golden Retriever. The female, Cowslip, had litters sired by a Tweed Water Spaniel and a red setter, and their progeny were bred both to black retrievers and among themselves. A bloodhound influence was later introduced.

Majoribanks, along with various family members who were also dedicated sportsmen, eventually created a distinctive strain of gifted retrievers. These dogs were not only attractive and talented, but because they were owned by prominent families, they were seen and eventually acquired by other wealthy sportsmen as they visited one another's estates for shooting parties. Lord Tweedmouth was reportedly fairly close with his dogs, but a few did leave to influence retrievers elsewhere. His family was well connected, and several of them maintained their own kennels that continued Lord Tweedmouth's lines. Lord Tweedmouth kept meticulous records of his dogs, but his records ended in 1890. The last two dogs mentioned were named Prim and Rose. His successors did not maintain records, so most of the breed's history during the subsequent two decades has been lost.

# New Occupations

The emergence of the Golden Retriever occurred at one of the most exciting times in the entire history of domestic dogs. Prior to the mid-1800s it was not uncommon for contests to be staged between fighting or coursing dogs, but gundogs were not included in such events. This changed in 1865 with the first trials for pointers and setters, and shortly thereafter, the first conformation dog shows. The interest the aristocracy showed in these events encouraged dog fanciers to participate. The need for an overseeing organization to register dogs and set competition rules became apparent, and in 1873 the Kennel Club (of England) was founded—by a retriever enthusiast, incidentally.

The first Goldens were exhibited in 1908 by Lord Harcourt of Culham Kennel. In these early days of retriever breeding, littermates could come in various colors and coat types, and although different strains

GOLD ⭐ STAR

Ch Noranby Campfire was the first Golden conformation champion, attaining the title of English Champion in 1913.

and types existed, they were all simply "Retrievers" as far as the Kennel Club was concerned. In 1913 the Kennel Club began registering them as varieties of Retrievers, so that Goldens were then shown as "Retrievers (Yellow or Golden)." This was simplified a few years later to "Retrievers (Golden)."

Being registered as varieties of a breed, rather than separate breeds, meant that dogs could be registered as whatever variety they most resembled, even if that meant that littermates having different coat colors or types might be registered or shown as different varieties. This proved to be unsatisfactory, and in 1916 retrievers from parents of different varieties were called "Interbred Retrievers," and only after they were bred back to one parental variety for three generations were the progeny registered as purebreds of that variety. This set the stage for defining pure breeds of retrievers, while still allowing, after three generations, the influx of genes from other retriever breeds. In fact, as recently as 1929, a yellow Labrador Retriever (FTCh Haylers Defender) was bred into the Golden Retriever breed, and many successful Goldens today descend from him. Eventually, the Kennel Club, as well as its American counterpart, the American Kennel Club, tightened their definitions of breeds.

Breed interest gradually grew and the Golden Retriever prospered in England. Goldens were making their names known in both the ring and

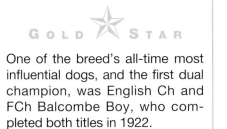

GOLD ★ STAR

One of the breed's all-time most influential dogs, and the first dual champion, was English Ch and FCh Balcombe Boy, who completed both titles in 1922.

field, and there was much anticipation of a steady increase in numbers and accomplishments. World War I caused a temporary setback, but the breed recovered quickly and was soon stronger than ever. World War II proved to be more devastating. Not only were all shows and trials canceled, but there was not enough food for kennels of large dogs, and many large breeds virtually disappeared from Britain. Fortunately, the Golden had some dedicated breeders who sacrificed in order to keep some core breeding stock going, and after the war, the Golden once again emerged as the golden child of the dog world. Breeders in other parts of the world also helped to keep the breed strong.

## American Gold

Almost certainly, the first Golden to come to North America came with one of Lord Tweedmouth's sons in the 1890s. Conflicting evidence exists as to whether Lady came with Archie Majoribanks to America or was born from an unidentified Golden female he brought with him. Either way, Lady was the dog immortalized in several photographs

*The first Golden in America is thought to have journeyed to Texas.*

*The wetlands of America's central flyway provided an ideal habitat in which the Golden could shine as a waterfowl retriever.*

from the time, and she can lay claim to being either the first Golden import to America or the first Golden born in America. There is also confusion about whether she had a litter while in America. Regardless, her offspring did not have a lasting influence on the breed in this country.

GOLD ★ STAR

Lomberdale Blondin was the first Golden registered with the American Kennel Club (AKC), in 1925.

The first AKC Champion, American and Canadian Ch Speedwell Pluto, was also the first Best in Show winner (1933).

In subsequent years, dogs of unmistakable Golden type were occasionally seen in the United States and Canada, but they were far from commonplace. The first kennel of note in North America—Gilnockie—began breeding Goldens in 1918. This was followed in 1928 by one of the most influential kennels—Rockhaven. The owner of Rockhaven, Colonel S. S. Magoffin, eventually acquired Gilnockie as well, but Magoffin's greatest influence was his part in founding the Golden Retriever Club of America (GRCA). This led to the American Kennel Club's official recognition of the Golden Retriever in 1932, five years after recognition by the Canadian Kennel Club.

Like many pure breeds, the Golden captured the hearts of dog enthusiasts eager to make their mark in the burgeoning dog show world. Dog shows in America were centered in the Northeast, so the Golden made strides as a showdog in the eastern United States. The Golden had a distinct advantage compared to many of the other new show breeds; it appealed just as much—in fact, more—to the many sportsmen of North America. Sporting Goldens found a new home around parts of the central United States, where bird hunting was a passion and a good retriever a necessity. This geographical difference in the opportunity to show versus hunt was, unfortunately, the first inkling of a split into show or working lines.

## Competition

In the ensuing years, the Golden made steady progress as it proved itself a worthy competitor in field trials, dogs shows, and in new areas: obedience and tracking trials. These trials afforded an outlet in which Golden breeders who had no access to hunting could test one aspect of their dogs' working ability. This created a new group of Golden owners and breeders: those who were not interested in showing, did not have the opportunity for hunting, but nonetheless appreciated competing in a performance venue.

Increased competition within each venue made it difficult for one dog to excel in every field. While the

GOLD ★ STAR

The first English and American Champion was Eng Am Ch Bingo of Yelme, who finished his American title in four shows, undefeated in the breed; he was also the first Golden to achieve All-Age status.

saying "Jack of All Trades, Master of All" still could be applied to the Golden, to be the best Master at any one trade began to require a dog bred for that job alone. Show, field, and obedience lines started to diverge, with serious breeders in each producing exceptional dogs for their purpose.

*Goldens also proved themselves on upland game birds, expanding their territory throughout drier areas of North America.*

GOLD ★ STAR

The very first GRCA National Specialty was held in 1940 and won by Beavertail Gay Lady.

The Golden had one more area in which it would prove exceptional: family pet. As more people saw and interacted with Goldens, many more elected to get one, not as any kind of competition dog, but as a family pet. In typical fashion, Goldens weren't content to be just another family dog; it was as though they set out to become the ultimate family companion. The greatest strides in the breed's popularity came because of its capabilities as a companion, and its numbers grew steadily.

*Goldens have found their strongest talent as loving, intelligent, and trustworthy family companions.*

# The Gold Rush

A new population of pet breeders arose, and this group eventually far outnumbered the original groups. Unfortunately, the pet breeders were largely unaware of the emerging recognition of hereditary health problems in the 1950s and 60s. They bred oblivious to the research undertaken and guidelines recommended by the Golden Retriever Club of America concerning crippling hip dysplasia or subsequent eye problems. The GRCA was instrumental in establishing the Orthopedic Foundation for Animals (OFA), but pet breeders were seldom informed or concerned about OFA clearances or any other health screening, a situation that would have dire consequences in the years to come.

The population of Goldens was now growing as never before. With increasing popularity, Goldens began to be included in movie roles and television commercials, a symbol of a wholesome family with an All-American dog (even if it was really British). If not every American was already aware of the Golden Retriever by the mid-seventies, they surely were when President Ford made a Golden Retriever named Liberty the First Dog. By that time, AKC registrations had reached almost 22,000 Goldens per year.

Any breed with that kind of popularity and exposure is perfect material for unethical breeders and puppy mills, and Goldens were now excelling at something they didn't want to be:

money-making puppy producers. In some cases, they were the victims of puppy mills churning out dogs to an unsuspecting public; in others, they were simply the pets of naïve backyard breeders unaware of the harm they were doing.

Even then, not every Golden had the temperament, health, or physical qualities that exemplified the breed; yet, these dogs were bred repeatedly, with no regard to the quality of the dogs produced or the lives they lived. Dogs with improper socialization, bad temperaments, and poor health were sold to people who didn't know the difference, and who, in turn, bred their poor-quality Goldens. As numbers grew and quality fell, prices also fell, and more people got Goldens on a whim, only to abandon them at the slightest problem.

At the end of World War II, fewer than 150 Goldens were registered with the AKC each year. In 1998 over 65,000 were registered. Lord Tweedmouth surely could never have foreseen the popularity and worldwide impact his breed would have throughout the twentieth century, but he even more certainly could not have imagined that this most noble and giving of dogs could ever be found peering from a cage at an animal shelter—a breed that had proven to be too good for its own good.

## Golden Rays

Today, the Golden remains a formidable force in every competitive

### GOLD NUGGET

**A Friend in Need**
Support Golden Retriever Rescue. If you can find room in your home and heart, consider adopting a rescue Golden as your next family member. Even if you cannot add a new permanent member, by volunteering as a foster home you can help nurse a homeless Golden back to physical or emotional health while it awaits a new permanent family. If you have reached your dog or emotional limit, you can still do your part with financial contributions or by joining the network of hardworking people who match dogs and people, canvass animal shelters for Goldens, or transport rescued dogs to their new homes. Even if you're not up to a full-fledged commitment, you can at least register with your local animal shelter and ask to be contacted when a Golden comes through their door. It's easy to love a Golden when everything is going well. The true test of your love for the breed is your ability to help when the chips are down.

event to which it has turned its attention. Despite too many uncommitted owners, the Golden Retriever retains a large core of responsible people totally in love with the breed and ready to help as many Goldens in trouble as possible. Goldens, too, have turned their attention to helping

*Today the Golden Retriever is more often found healing hearts and sharing its golden personality with family, friends, and anyone who will stop and share a golden moment.*

cles, and most of all, use air scenting to pinpoint the location of a hidden person. National and local canine search and rescue teams are available for local emergencies, and may also be prepared to fly across the country in the cases of disasters. Golden Retrievers have shown they can retrieve lost people every bit as well as fallen birds.

### Therapy Dogs

Therapy dogs visit hospitals, nursing homes, mental health facilities, prisons, and other places where they can provide people with uncon-

people in trouble. They have once again reinvented themselves as extraordinary service dogs, demonstrating that these dogs are truly golden.

Most Goldens today never enter any competition or win a single ribbon. Why should they? They've already won the biggest prize of all—their family's hearts. Some Goldens don't stop there, though; they go on to save lives, guide futures, and heal hearts. Golden Retrievers excel at many tasks, but certainly none more noble than those in which they help people in need.

### Search and Rescue

Search and Rescue (SAR) teams may search over miles of wilderness to find a lost child or through tons of rubble to discover a buried victim. SAR Goldens must respond reliably to commands, negotiate precarious footing, follow a trail and locate arti-

G O L D  ★  S T A R

When Golden Retriever lovers learned the story of Duke, a Golden with extensive injuries suggestive of being dragged behind a car, they rallied to raise money toward helping his recovery. So successful were they that not only did Duke recover fully (and in true golden-hearted forgiveness and trust, later earned his CGC award), but enough extra money was available to set up the Duke Fund, which is now used to help other Goldens in need. Tax-deductible donations can be sent to the Duke Fund, Golden Retrievers in Cyberspace, 861 Somerset Drive, Sunnyvale, CA 94087-2224. For more information, go to http://www.golden-retriever.com/duke-fund.html.

GOLD ★ STAR

A Golden ski patrol dog named Doc had already saved several lost hikers, but his biggest rescue came when he dug out an avalanche victim buried under five feet of snow in an area far from where human searchers were looking—and with time running out. His grateful rescuee now sports a tattoo of Doc next to his heart.

## GOLD NUGGET

### On the Slopes
Golden Retrievers are among the most popular breeds for avalanche rescue at ski resorts. They spend most days riding the ski lift, patrolling with their handlers, and acting as goodwill ambassadors, but when a skier is covered by snow, they can cover the same area in 30 minutes that it would take an entire human team eight hours to probe.

ditional love, motivation to communicate, entertainment, or just somebody warm and cuddly to hug. Therapy dogs must be meticulously well mannered and well groomed, and above all, friendly and utterly trustworthy. If someone grabs, yells at, or hugs a therapy dog too tightly, the dog must remain gentle and unperturbed. The Certified Therapy Dog letters are among the proudest a dog can attain. The Golden Retriever, with its optimistic outlook and uncanny knack for understanding human emotions, has warmed many hearts, dried many tears, and opened many arms—a true therapist in a fur coat.

## Golden Aides

Golden Retrievers are among the most popular breeds for helping people with mental and physical challenges. It's no surprise; the ideal helping dog is one that is intelligent, eager to please, yet able to think on its own. It needs to be confident and personable, and of adequate strength to guide or pull a person. The desire and ability to retrieve is certainly a plus, good health is a necessity, and good looks are a nice bonus.

**Helping the physically impaired:** Golden and Labrador Retrievers are the most popular breeds for helping people with physical disabilities. This assistance can take the form of pulling a person in a wheelchair, picking up dropped objects, getting objects off high shelves, opening doors, and pushing a 911 button in case of emergency.

Other service dogs specialize in alerting when a person is about to have a seizure. Exactly how these dogs become aware of an impending seizure even before the person knows one is coming is unknown, but it's thought that the dog smells a change in body chemistry associated with changes in brain activity.

## G O L D   N U G G E T

**Contact these organizations for more information about service dogs:**

Assistance Dogs International
C/O Freedom Service Dogs
P.O. Box 150217
Lakewood, CO 80215-0217
Tel: (610) 869-4902
http://www.assistance-dogs-
  intl.org

Delta Society National Service
  Dog Center
289 Perimeter Road East
Renton, WA 98055
Tel: (800) 869-6898
E-mail: info@deltasociety.org
http://www.deltasociety.org

Canine Companions for
  Independence
P.O. Box 446
Santa Rosa, CA 95402-0446
Tel: (800) 572-2275
E-mail: info@caninecompanions.
  org
http://www.caninecompanions.
  org

Paws With a Cause
4646 South Division
Wayland, MI 49348
Tel: (800) 253-PAWS
E-mail: paws@alliance.net
http://www.ismi.net/paws

**Start your search for SAR information at:**

Search and Rescue Dog
  Resources
4 Orchard Way North
Rockville, MD 20854
Tel: (301) 762-7217
E-mail: sardogs@nasar.org
http://www.nasar.org/canine/
  dogdir.shtml

American Rescue Dog Association
P.O. Box 151
Chester, NY 10918
Tel: (715) 545-2220
http://www.ardainc.org/xcontent.
  htm

These dogs provide a measure of safety and confidence for their people; still other dogs provide safety once a seizure has occurred, lying next to the person until it has subsided. Seizure dogs must know the difference between friend and foe, allowing helpers to approach the victim, while discouraging those with bad intentions.

**Helping the visually impaired:** The working guide dog is expected to take directional instructions from the handler, locate specified objects such as curbs, doors, and steps, stop at obstacles, changes in elevation, or dangerous traffic situations, and reasonably ignore distractions during its work and even commands from the handler if they would result in danger to the handler. They give their visually impaired handlers mobility, confidence, independence, and love.

In recent years, Golden and Labrador Retrievers, as well crosses between the two, have made up the majority of guide dogs. Some guide dog facilities breed their own dogs, whereas others accept donated puppies that pass certain very stringent criteria. Most facilities rely on puppy raisers to provide a home environment, well-rounded socialization, and basic obedience to youngsters. The puppies then go to the school for formal training when they are between 12 and 18 months of age. Not all dogs graduate, but those that do have a full life ahead of them.

**Helping the hearing impaired:** Dogs can also provide confidence and assistance for hearing-impaired people. Although most dogs for the deaf are small dogs rescued from humane organizations, Golden Retrievers have also been trained to do the same job. Dogs at the lowest (Novice) level are trained to alert the person to a smoke alarm, the person's name being called, and the alarm clock. A slightly more highly trained dog (Home Level) alerts the person to the doorbell, telephone, and oven timer. The certified hearing dog responds to these same sounds but is also extensively socialized and obedience-trained so that it is dependable in public as well as in the home. As such, it meets the Americans with Disabilities Act standard and is allowed in all public places.

G OLD ★ S TAR

When an assistance Golden named Heidi saved her person's life by lying down abruptly on his chest when his lungs had filled from pneumonia, not only did she add this skill to her list of commands, but she also demonstrated through later medical studies that dogs could effectively clear people's lungs.

## Contraband Detection

Some Golden Retrievers have become integral members of police departments by sniffing out drugs and explosives. No machine has ever been found that can compete with the dog's sense of smell, and when called upon, the Golden Retriever has demonstrated it can use its nose with the best of them! However, Goldens aren't as popular for this as some other breeds because they are too easygoing to be all-around police dogs, and too large to negotiate the small spaces sometimes involved in searching for contraband.

Although developed as a dog of the aristocracy, with an uncanny ability to brave rough conditions and retrieve downed birds, the Golden Retriever has proven time and again that it is a dog of the people, with an uncanny ability to brave tough times and retrieve fallen spirits. Surely Lord Tweedmouth would approve.

# Chapter Two
# The Gold Standard

Goldens can be beautiful in many ways. The main one, of course, is through their golden personalities. For the hunter, the most beautiful Golden is the one that has proven itself in the field as a reliable and athletic retriever. To the true Golden enthusiast, the most beautiful Golden combines beauty of temperament, function, and appearance.

Golden Retrievers look as they do because they are built a certain way to do a certain job. The breed originated as a working breed, with function as its first priority. But the breed's founders also had an esthetic sense for the dog they had molded, and these points of beauty were valued in defining a dog as a Golden Retriever—in other words, in defining the breed's type.

The breed standard is an attempt to describe the ideal Golden Retriever, with the idea that a dog that is built right can function well, without ignoring the finer points essential to the unique beauty of the breed. The breed standard is the measuring stick by which Goldens are judged in the show ring. The Golden Retriever originated in Britain; because of that, the standard used to judge the breed there is also the one used to judge the breed throughout much of the rest of the world.

## The British Standard

**General Appearance:** Symmetrical, balanced, active, powerful, level mover; sound with kindly expression.

**Characteristics:** Biddable, intelligent and possessing natural working ability.

GOLD ★ STAR

Goldens such as American Canadian Ch and OTCh Bonnie Island Gold Rush Carla, WC, Canadian WC, American and Canadian UDTX are a testament to the standard's recognition of a versatile dog.

*The Golden Retriever standard describes a functional working retriever.*

*Ultimate beauty lies in perfection of form, ability, and character.*

**Temperament:** Kindly, friendly and confident.

**Coat:** Flat or wavy with good feathering, dense water-resisting undercoat.

**Colour:** Any shade of gold or cream, neither red nor mahogany. A few white hairs on chest only, permissible.

**Size:** Height at withers: dogs: 56–61 cm (22–24 in); bitches: 51–56 cm (20–22 in).

In the United States, the Golden Retriever is evaluated with the far more detailed American Kennel Club Standard.

**Note:** Comments have been added for clarification at the end of each section, but these are not part of the standard and are only a personal interpretation of the wording.

# The American Standard

**General Appearance:** A symmetrical, powerful, active dog, sound and well put together, not clumsy nor long in the leg, displaying a kindly expression and possessing a personality that is eager, alert and self-confident. Primarily a hunting dog, he should be shown in hard working condition.

Overall appearance, balance, gait and purpose to be given more emphasis than any of his component parts. Faults—Any departure from the described ideal shall be considered faulty to the degree to which it interferes with the breed's purpose or is contrary to breed character.

*Comment: The Golden Retriever is more than a sum of its parts. If you* had only two sentences with which to evaluate or describe a Golden, the first two sentences of this section would do the job nicely.

**Size, Proportion, Substance:** Males 23–24 inches in height at withers; females 21½–22½ inches. Dogs up to one inch above or below standard size should be proportionately penalized. Deviation in height of more than one inch from the standard shall disqualify. Length from breastbone to point of buttocks slightly greater than height at withers in ratio of 12:11. Weight for dogs 65–75 pounds; bitches 55–65 pounds.

*Comment: The standard is fairly strict concerning size because a smaller dog may have difficulty carrying heavy game or jumping large obstacles; a larger dog may crowd a boat or blind. The Golden Retriever's torso is very slightly longer than tall; too short a body and the front and rear legs may interfere with each other when trotting; too long a body may stress the back.*

**Head:** Broad in skull, slightly arched laterally and longitudinally without prominence of frontal bones (forehead) or occipital bones. Stop well defined but not abrupt. Foreface deep and wide, nearly as long as skull. Muzzle—straight in profile, blending smooth and strongly into skull; when viewed in profile or from above, slightly deeper and wider at stop than at tip. No heaviness in flews. Removal of whiskers is permitted but not preferred. Eyes—friendly and intelligent in expression, medium large with dark, close-fitting rims, set well apart and reasonably deep in sockets. Color preferably dark brown; medium brown acceptable. Slant eyes and narrow, triangular eyes detract from correct expression and are to be faulted. No white or haw visible when looking straight ahead. Dogs showing evidence of

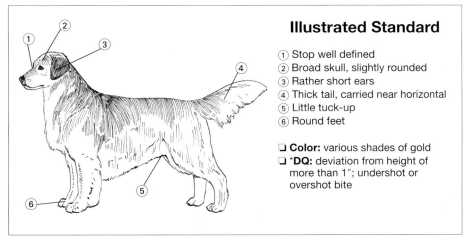

## Illustrated Standard

1 Stop well defined
2 Broad skull, slightly rounded
3 Rather short ears
4 Thick tail, carried near horizontal
5 Little tuck-up
6 Round feet

❏ **Color:** various shades of gold
❏ ***DQ:** deviation from height of more than 1″; undershot or overshot bite

*DQ = disqualification

functional abnormality of eyelids or eyelashes (such as, but not limited to, trichiasis, entropion, ectropion, or distichiasis) are to be excused from the ring. Ears—rather short with front edge attached well behind and just above the eye and falling close to cheek. When pulled forward, tip of ear should just cover the eye. Low, hound-like ear set to be faulted. Nose—black or brownish black, though fading to a lighter shade in cold weather not serious. Pink nose or one seriously lacking in pigmentation to be faulted. Teeth—scissors bite, in which the outer side of the lower incisors touches the inner side of the upper incisors. Undershot or overshot bite is a disqualification. Misalignment of teeth (irregular placement of incisors) or a level bite (incisors meet each other edge to edge) is undesirable, but not to be confused with undershot or overshot. Full dentition. Obvious gaps are serious faults.

*Comment: The Golden's head gives it more than just a pretty face. It is strong, but not coarse; rounded, but not domed—all in all, a moderate head without extremes. The deep, wide foreface gives it the jaw strength to hold heavy objects without needing to crush them. Overly pendulous lips could interfere with picking up game, and are also more likely to collect feathers. Besides, the longer and heavier the flews, the more the drool factor! The whiskers (more properly, "vibrissae") are important sensory receptors and, as such, should not be cut. Anecdotal stories of dogs in the field report that dogs without vibrissae are more likely to scratch their faces in thick brush.*

*The eye set affords a wide visual field. An eye set too shallowly in its socket is prone to corneal abrasions, but one set too deeply is prone to entropion (in which the lid turns in toward the eye). A close-fitting lid is less likely to collect seeds and other debris, and is also less likely to be affected by various lid disorders (see page 86). Eye color, while not related to function, is a matter of esthetics and breed type; along with shape, it helps to impart the sweet, intelligent expression that is the hallmark of the breed.*

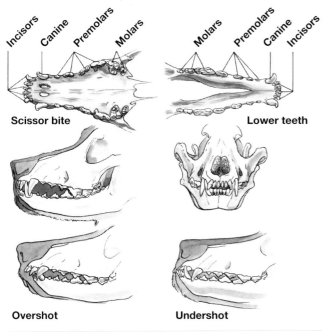

**Incisors  Canine  Premolars  Molars**     **Molars  Premolars  Canine  Incisors**

**Scissor bite**                **Lower teeth**

**Overshot**                **Undershot**

*Canine dentition.*

The Golden's ear is also designed for a purpose. The flap protects the ear canal from seeds, debris, wind, and water, but is not so long that it is easily injured or hinders ventilation of the canal. A higher-set ear (and canal) is less likely to be immersed in water when the dog is swimming.

Most Goldens have dark noses when young, but many of them tend to lighten every winter, and never quite darken up again to their original shade. This is typical of many breeds of dogs with light coat color; even so, these dogs will retain dark lips and eye rims, and the nose is usually still dark around the edges. A true liver or pink nose is different. Liver is not typical for the breed, and pink indicates a lack of pigment and susceptibility to sunburn.

Just as in humans, proper dental occlusion is not only esthetically pleasing, but essential to good dental health (see page 63). In the Golden, it has the added importance of contributing to a firm grip on retrieved objects. Missing teeth may weaken the gripping power of the mouth. Most missing teeth are the small premolars, however, which singularly probably have little effect.

**Neck, Topline, Body:** Neck medium long, merging gradually into well laid back shoulders, giving sturdy, muscular appearance. No throatiness. Backline strong and level from withers to slightly sloping croup, whether standing or moving. Sloping backline, roach or sway back, flat or steep croup to be faulted. Body—well balanced, short coupled, deep

*The Golden's head is functional as well as esthetically pleasing.*

through the chest. Chest—between forelegs at least as wide as a man's closed hand including thumb, with well developed forechest. Brisket extends to elbow. Ribs—long and well sprung but not barrel shaped, extending well towards hindquarters. Loin—short, muscular, wide and deep, with very little tuck-up. Slab-sidedness, narrow chest, lack of depth in brisket, excessive tuck-up to be faulted. Tail—well set on, thick and muscular at the base, following the natural line of the croup. Tail bones extend to, but not below, the point of hock. Carried with merry action, level or with some moderate upward curve; never curled over back nor between legs.

*Comments: A neck that is too short may hinder the dog's ability to reach down to pick up game on the ground; an overly long neck lacks strength. A neck that flows smoothly into the withers is an indication of strong muscular attachments and usually accompanies shoulders that are well laid back; that is, a front assembly in which the top of the scapula is angled well back toward the rear of the dog. Viewed from the side, the neck blends into the backline, which should form a straight level line between the withers and croup. The backline transfers energy from the rear of the dog to the front, so it cannot afford to be weak. If the croup (area over the pelvis) is too level, the rear leg may not move forward sufficiently or as freely as it optimally could; if it's too steep, the rear leg may not thrust backward sufficiently. The tail is the banner of the Golden Retriever; its merry wagging action bears testament to the Golden's disposition.*

*At first, the descriptions that the body should be slightly longer than tall and that the dog be short-coupled seem at odds; however, this simply states that the length in body should not originate from an excessively long area between the rib cage and croup. This point is made clear by the descriptions that the rib cage should extend well toward the hindquarters and that the loin should be short. Further, there should be no significant tuck-up—that is, no greyhoundlike waist. The rib cage supplies ample room for the internal organs; it must be able to expand and contract to accommodate the expansion and contraction of the lungs. A rib cage that is either too flat or too rounded does not do so as optimally as a rib cage that is moderately round. In addition, too narrow a rib cage does not provide the buoyancy needed for swimming; too wide a rib cage interferes with the free movement of the forelimbs.*

**Forequarters:** Muscular, well coordinated with hindquarters and capable of free movement. Shoulder blades—long and well laid back with upper tips fairly close together at withers. Upper arms—appear about the same length as the blades, setting the elbows back beneath the upper tip of the blades, close to the ribs without looseness. Legs—viewed from the front, straight with good bone, but not to the point of coarseness. Pasterns—short and strong, sloping slightly with no suggestion of weakness. Dewclaws on forelegs may be removed, but are

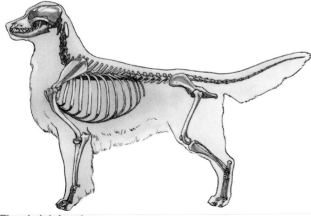

*The skeletal system.*

normally left on. Feet—medium size, round, compact, and well knuckled, with thick pads. Excess hair may be trimmed to show natural size and contour. Splayed or hare feet to be faulted.

*Comments: The forequarters carry most of the Golden's weight and provide most of the swimming propulsion. The forelegs must provide a strong, straight column of support, but they must also be able to absorb shock, which is achieved by having pasterns that slope slightly forward. Splayed feet in which the toes lack support are weak; hare feet in which the toes are long and narrow are more prone to injury and do not provide adequate swimming power.*

**Hindquarters:** Broad and strongly muscled. Profile of croup slopes slightly; the pelvic bone slopes at a slightly greater angle (approximately 30 degrees from horizontal). In a natural stance, the femur joins the pelvis at approximately a 90-degree angle; stifles—well bent; hocks—well let down with short, strong rear pasterns. Feet as in front. Legs—straight when viewed from rear. Cow-hocks, spread hocks, and sickle hocks to be faulted.

*Comments: The rear quarters provide most of the propulsion while on land. If the angles are too straight, the gait will be stilted; if they are too extreme, the muscles will have to work too hard to support the dog's weight throughout the stride, and the dog will tire easily. Sickle hocks prevent the joint between the second thigh and hock from extending*

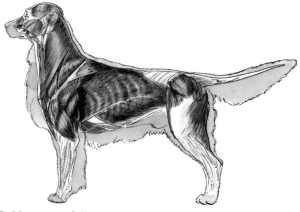
*Golden musculature.*

*fully. Hock joints that point in or out interfere with the straight and direct transfer of power from foot to pelvis.*

**Coat:** Dense and water-repellent with good undercoat. Outer coat firm and resilient, neither coarse nor silky, lying close to body; may be straight or wavy. Untrimmed natural ruff; moderate feathering on back of forelegs and on underbody; heavier feathering on front of neck, back of thighs and underside of tail. Coat on head, paws, and front of legs is short and even. Excessive length, open coats, and limp, soft coats are very undesirable. Feet may be trimmed and stray hairs neatened, but the natural appearance of coat or outline should not be altered by cutting or clipping.

*Comments: The real beauty of the Golden's coat lies in its ability to shield the dog from cold, water, and brambles. Too little coat won't provide sufficient protection; too much coat can become weighted down*

*The ability to move effortlessly is an essential aspect of proper conformation.*

*or entangled with water and debris or cause overheating. The outer coat is tough and encapsulates the dog's body in a protective sheath; too soft or silky a coat doesn't provide sufficient protection or the dirt-shedding ability of a harsher coat. The undercoat is short, dense, and somewhat oily, providing waterproofing and insulation. Males often carry slightly fuller coats, particularly the ruff on the neck. As coat quantity is affected by climate and seasonal shedding, it is of less importance than coat quality.*

**Color:** Rich, lustrous golden of various shades. Feathering may be lighter than rest of coat. With the exception of graying or whitening of face or body due to age, any white marking, other than a few white hairs on the chest, should be penalized according to its extent. Allowable light shadings are not to be confused with white markings. Predominant body color which is either extremely pale or extremely dark is undesirable. Some latitude should be given to the light puppy whose coloring shows promise of deepening with maturity. Any noticeable area of black or other off-color hair is a serious fault.

*Comments: Gold comes in many shades, but it should not be so dark as to approach red nor so light as to approach off-white. It is not unusual for gold dogs of any breed to sometimes have areas of black hairs, varying in size from a few hairs to a large splotch. Such areas arise from a somatic mutation, in which the DNA of one embryonic cell mutates from gold to black. All subsequent cells derived from this mutated cell will be black, and the earlier the mutation occurs during development, the more cells that one cell gives rise to, and the larger the black spot will be. Somatic mutations are neither hereditary nor harmful—think of them as birthmarks.*

**Gait:** When trotting, gait is free, smooth, powerful and well coordinated, showing good reach. Viewed from any position, legs turn neither in nor out, nor do feet cross or interfere with each other. As speed increases, feet tend to converge toward center line of balance. It is recommended that dogs be shown on a loose lead to reflect true gait.

*Comment: The optimal gait should allow the Golden to take long strides with a minimum of exertion. If the strides are too short, the dog will have to pump its legs more to get anywhere; if they are too long, it has to put too much energy into each stride. In fact, recent evidence suggests that an extremely long stride of the foreleg actually imposes a braking force on forward momentum. Viewed from the front or rear, the feet tend to move closer to one another as the dog's speed increases; otherwise, the dog would sway from side to side as it ran.*

**Temperament:** Friendly, reliable, and trustworthy. Quarrelsomeness or hostility toward other dogs or people in normal situations, or an unwarranted show of timidity or nervousness, is not in keeping with Golden Retriever character. Such actions should be penalized according to their significance.

*Comment: The most beautiful, sound, functional Golden Retriever ever created is no credit to its breed without the most essential trait of all: the renowned Golden Retriever character. The ideal Golden Retriever is a versatile and adaptive dog, calm around the house, playful when the opportunity arises, intense when on*

GOLD ★ STAR

Proving that show dogs can do it all, BIS BISS Ch Elysian's Lil Leica Reprint, UDT, MH, WCX, SDHF, VCX, OD is the first, and so far, only sporting dog to win a Best in Show and earn the MH title—not to mention all the others.

*the job, and always amiable, sensible, and responsive. Overemphasis on one dimension can lead to a dog that, on one extreme, is always in overdrive, and on the other, is too laid back to get the job done.*

**Disqualifications:** Deviation in height of more than one inch from standard either way.

Undershot or overshot bite.

*Comments: Disqualifications render the dog ineligible for conformation competition. These disqualifications are those specific to Golden Retrievers. The AKC has other disqualifications that pertain to all breeds (see page 131).*

No dog—not even a Golden Retriever—is perfect. The flaws of every dog must be evaluated in terms of their effect on the dog's ability to function or on its adherence to breed type. Not every dog has to be a show dog, but if you plan to compete with your dog in conformation or plan to breed your dog, you need to do an honest evaluation against the standard, and then love your dog just the same regardless of how it measures up!

# Chapter Three

# All That Glitters Is Not Gold

It's not hard to find a Golden Retriever, even a good Golden Retriever. But if you want one that represents the breed at its finest, you can hedge your bet by choosing your source carefully. To do that, you need to know how to tell good breeders from bad breeders, and good Goldens from great Goldens.

## Finding a 24-Karat Golden

Prospective Golden Retriever owners have various goals. Some want a reliable hunting partner, some a competitive show dog, and some an outstanding obedience competitor, each of which will require looking in slightly different places. Others simply want a healthy, personable, attractive family companion.

No matter what your goals are with your dog, the first priority is that

*Be forewarned: if you go to look at a Golden puppy, chances are you won't come home empty-handed!*

it be as healthy as possible, so health screening goes without saying in all cases. And no matter what your goals, you'll be better off buying from a good breeder than a bad one.

Good breeders:
• Are familiar with and screen for Golden Retriever health concerns such as hip and elbow dysplasia, subaortic stenosis, and eye anomalies.
• Won't allow pups to leave until they are at least eight weeks old.
• Can compare their dogs to the breed standard feature by feature.
• Charge neither bargain basement nor an exorbitant price for puppies.
• Have photos and pedigrees of both parents and other relatives.
• Breed sparingly and dedicate their breeding efforts to only one or two breeds.
• Belong to a local or national Golden Retriever club.
• Are involved in some sort of Golden competitive activity or service.
• Ask prospective owners lots of questions about their past history with dogs, their facilities, family,

lifestyle, and expectations for their new dog, and point out that even Golden Retrievers aren't for everyone.

• Require that should prospective owners ever have to relinquish the dog, the breeder gets first refusal.

• Provide a medical history, pedigree, registration slip, and written care instructions with each puppy.

## Finding a Golden Retriever Companion

Most people seeking a new Golden don't want a hunting or competition dog, just a new best friend. Their most common sources are newspaper ads, friends, pet stores, hobby breeders, and rescue. Of these, hobby breeders and rescue organizations should be your first choices.

Hobby breeders are people who have made producing superior Golden Retrievers a main focus of their lives. They will usually have proven their dogs in some form of competition, whether conformation, obedience, or field, and will also have screened their breeding stock for hereditary health problems. In so doing, they have probably spent far more money than they could ever hope to recover, even by charging somewhat more for their pups. Despite their efforts, not every pup will turn out to be competition quality, although all will have profited from the breeder's knowledge of genetics and puppy care. These "pet-quality" pups still need good homes, and are usually made available for a very reasonable fee. Good hobby breeders will screen prospective pet homes no less diligently than their other prospective homes, and will expect you to keep them abreast of your pup's progress and come to them with your problems, just like all of their puppy buyers. One word of caution, however: A dog bred from obedience or field competition lines may be more energetic than the average family can handle.

Hobby breeders are sometimes hard to find, though, since most don't advertise in the paper. A good starting place is the Golden Retriever Club of America. You can also look in dog magazines, and especially Golden Retriever magazines, or at kennel pages on the Web. Joining a Golden Retriever discussion group on the Internet is a good way to let breeders know you are looking. Try to visit prospective breeders personally and see for yourself how puppies and adults look and act, and how puppies are being raised.

**Age:** Most people consider only a puppy when they set out to get a dog, but that's not always the best idea. No one can deny that a puppy is cute and fun, but a puppy is much like a baby; you can't ever be too busy to walk, feed, supervise, or clean—and clean and clean. If you work away from home, have limited patience or heirloom rugs, or if you demand a competition or breeding-quality dog, an older puppy or adult may be a better choice. Breeders may have adult dogs available that would relish the chance to live as a

*An older Golden makes an ideal choice if you prefer to save your home and sanity—and offer a loving home to a dog in need.*

pampered pet. They may have adults that simply didn't win as much in the ring as anticipated, or that have not proven to be good producers, or that don't get along with their other dogs. They may be helping to place a dog for a family that can no longer keep it through no fault of the dog's. Such dogs are often already housebroken and obedience-trained. Although they will doubtless miss their former family, most Goldens are very adaptable and easily adopt a new family.

**Rescue Dogs:** Don't forget the many "rescue" Goldens in search of a new home. They come in all descriptions and have varied histories, but the typical rescue Golden is a young adult whose human family found out they weren't up to owning an energetic dog. Most of these dogs are just young Goldens acting like young Goldens; they need only to become part of a family who understands and appreciates their exuberance and need for mental and physical stimulation. A few come from traumatic backgrounds or may even be atypical Goldens; these dogs are best adopted by experienced Golden owners.

Before adopting a rescue dog, find out as much as you can about its background, the reason it was given up, how it relates to men, women, children, and other pets, and any temperament or health problems it may have. You may feel guilty looking at a dog in need with a critical eye, but you are doing that dog no favor at all if you can't cope with it any better than its former owners could. Good rescue groups will carefully match prospective adoptees with their new homes, increasing their chances of finding a home for life. Golden Retriever rescue groups usually have Goldens that have been screened for health and temperament problems, but the best organizations are as picky about prospective homes as the best breeders are.

### Finding a Golden Retriever Hunting Partner

Golden Retrievers have been bred for a long time to retrieve, and almost all of them can be easily trained to be adequate, or even very good, hunting retrievers. Few, however, can be exceptional hunting retrievers unless they come from a recent background of proven field dogs. If regular hunting or field trial competition is an important goal, you'll need to start a hunt of your own. The GRCA, retriever field magazines, Internet groups, and local field clubs are good places to start. Attending a retriever trial is a great way to see dogs in action and meet serious owners and breeders, but be sure to wait until after they've finished competing before you inundate them with questions.

Study the requirements (page 147) of the different hunting titles so you can appreciate the degree of accomplishments they represent. At least one parent of your prospective

*Look to the parents for the dogs their puppies will become.*

dog should have had at least the level of competency you hope to achieve with your dog. When both parents have advanced hunting titles, you may have to get in line for a pup! You should understand that if you have little experience with training or trialing a retriever, you may not be the breeder's first choice unless you agree to have the dog trained by a professional, or agree to work with the breeder in training the dog. Good breeders hope all of their puppies will blossom into fine dogs that represent their breeding at its best, so they want to make sure the puppy they sell you has the opportunity to live up to its full potential.

## Finding a Golden Retriever Show Dog

Show-bred Goldens are the result of generations of selection based upon extremely competitive show wins. It's hard enough to produce a good show dog even with the best of pedigrees; it's nearly impossible to do so by accident. Your prospective show dog's parents should ideally both be AKC Champions, and the pedigree should have a high percentage of champions. Don't be particularly influenced by titles or wins of dogs further removed than grandparents.

Contact the GRCA and ask for a list of breeders and local clubs. Contact the AKC and find out when a dog show, or preferably a Golden Retriever specialty show, will be held in your area. A specialty show is a prestigious show in which only

Golden Retrievers compete, and that attracts especially good competition. The GRCA National Specialty is the premier event in the United States, attracting hundreds of competing Golden Retrievers from the finest breeders around the country. Not only can you meet more breeders at large specialties, but you can also get a better idea of the particular look of Golden you prefer and what traits are most important to you. Often, breeders will have puppies for sale with them at a specialty or large show, but if you are really serious about finding the best show prospect, you should usually fight the urge to bring one home. It's better to find dogs that you really like and wait for them to have puppies than to first fall for a puppy and then hope it has a good background.

You should subscribe to a Golden Retriever magazine, where dogs from around the country are highlighted (see Useful Addresses and Literature, page 191). You may find yourself drawn to dogs from a breeder on the other side of the country who can send you videos of the parents and puppies. All else being equal, it's usually best to get a dog you've seen in the flesh from a local breeder who will be available to show you the ropes when you start showing.

## Finding a Golden Retriever Obedience Competitor

You don't have to look far to find a Golden that can compete, and even excel, in the obedience ring. Goldens from many backgrounds have completed CD, CDX, and UD obedience titles (see page 136). Earning such titles is considered a lifetime achievement for dogs of most breeds, but for many Goldens they're simply a warm-up for an OTCh (obedience trial championship). If you have aspirations of joining this highest echelon of the obedience world, you'll do best to search for a Golden specifically bred to excel at precision obedience. Higher-caliber obedience dogs tend to be very active, more so than the average Golden, so think carefully before blithely deciding you want to take this direction.

Contact the GRCA and ask for breeders of OTCh Goldens. Contact the AKC for the name of an obedience club near you and for locations of upcoming local obedience trials. Talk to handlers of Goldens that perform well, but wait until they have finished competing before asking questions. Get to meet the dogs away from the trial and see if this is the level of energy you enjoy. Your prospective obedience pup's parents should both have advanced obedience degrees.

Whatever your needs, know what you're looking for and don't hesitate to make your wishes known to the breeder. Being honest will be the best route for you, the breeder, and the dog. And keep in mind that there's no such thing as the "chance of a lifetime" litter, puppy, or dog, although chances are, whatever dog you choose will be a once-in-a-lifetime friend.

# Puppy Checklist

Even if you have no competitive goals, remember the essentials of any good Golden: good health, temperament, and looks.

## Health

For health, ask about longevity and health (and health clearances) of your potential pup's ancestors. Don't discount a line with some problems, as no line of dogs is perfect, and besides, some other breeders may simply not be as honest in disclosing problems. A good breeder will have either OFA (Orthopedic Foundation for Animals) or PennHIP hip dysplasia clearance, a heart clearance for subaortic stenosis, and a recent— within the last year and a half— CERF eye clearance. An OFA elbow clearance and veterinary certificate of normal thyroid function and lack of allergies or seizures is a definite plus. No matter how much research you do into the background of any puppy, there is no guarantee that your dog will live a long and healthy life, but why not go with the odds and choose a dog from the healthiest background possible?

Look at the pups. Are they being raised in sanitary conditions? Do they have their puppy vaccinations? Have they been checked or treated for internal parasites? Avoid pups that:
• are excessively dirty or soiled with feces.
• are covered with fleas or ticks.
• are missing hair.
• have crusted or reddened skin.
• are coughing, sneezing, or vomiting.

- have discharge from the eyes, ears, or nose.
- are red or irritated around the anus.
- have diarrhea.
- are thin or potbellied.
- have pale gums.
- are apathetic, lethargic, shy, or hostile.
- are dehydrated; test for dehydration by picking up a fold of skin and releasing it. The skin should "pop" back into place.

## Temperament

For temperament, again consider the essentials of the Golden Retriever standard. The Golden Retriever should be eager, alert and self-confident. It's human nature to go for the extremes in temperament,

**GOLD NUGGET**

OFA rates hips as Normal (with Excellent rated better than Good), Transitional (with Fair rated better than Borderline), and Dysplastic (with Mild rated better than Moderate, and both rated better than Severe). Elbow certification is either Normal or Dysplastic (see page 79 for more information about hip and elbow dysplasia).

but for most family companions you're better off choosing the pup that is neither the boldest nor shyest in the litter. Many people who can't decide, let the puppy pick them. It's hard to say no to a little pup that

*Some choices are just impossible.*

toddles over to say hello and ends up falling asleep in your lap. Of course, you may be in big trouble if you end up with a whole lapfull!

By eight weeks of age, most Golden puppies should be curious about their surroundings; while they may show some caution, they should still be willing to investigate. A puppy that freezes in place or always heads home may not have the self-confidence of the typical Golden. Most puppies should also tend to follow you, especially if you call. A puppy that consistently ignores you may be too independent. It's a good sign if the pup chases and even retrieves a rolled ball or tossed toy, but some Goldens develop the retrieving urge only at a much later age.

Consider your own lifestyle and personality. The mischievous, high-energy pup is always enticing, and usually great fun as an adult, but also usually a lot more work. Such a dog would be a good choice as an obedience prospect, but not for a working family. The laid-back Golden that is happiest to rest its head on your arm might be a good choice for a less active household, but not for a competition, obedience, or field dog. It's difficult to evaluate personalities in the short time you will be with the puppies, so consider carefully the breeder's opinions and suggestions.

## Looks

For looks, consider the essentials of the Golden Retriever standard. The Golden is a powerful, athletic dog, neither clumsy nor lanky, with a soft, kindly expression and golden coat of medium length. Your criteria will be more stringent if your pup is destined for a show career; in this case you should rely on the advice of the breeder, who will know better than anyone how dogs from that line mature.

Golden Retriever puppies are like little tanks. They trundle along on short, wide, moving legs with much choppier movement than they will have as adults. They change so much it's difficult to have hard rules about what to look for, but in general, bad movement from the front or rear as a puppy only gets worse, but side movement tends to get better. Angulation often gets straighter with maturity, and is usually straightest in young adults, after which it may increase again.

Golden pups are born light and darken with age; a very light pup may turn into a good golden shade, whereas a very dark pup may be almost red as an adult. The ear color is often a clue as to what the adult color will be. Pigment of the nose, eye rims, and feet pads starts off light and should be quite dark by seven weeks. If not, it will usually only get lighter again with age. Small white markings in young puppies may go away, but by seven weeks they should be almost gone if they are going to vanish.

If you want a male for conformation (or breeding), be sure he has both testicles descended into the

*The pup you pick will be the best—no matter which one it is.*

scrotum by the time you take him home. They should both be down by eight weeks of age, although some may be as late as sixteen weeks—or, in very rare cases longer—but don't bank on it!

The younger the dog, the more difficult it is to predict how it will look and move as an adult. This means that if you really want a surefire winner, your best bet is to buy an adult, perhaps even one that has already won a few points.

Finally, remember: There is only one irrefutable truism about picking a new Golden Retriever: No matter which one you pick, it will turn out to be the best one!

## Chapter Four

# Diets Worth Their Weight in Gold

Your Golden's performance, health, and longevity depend, in part, upon what you choose to feed him. Because most dogs are usually fed one type of food, choosing the best diet is even more important and intimidating. Understandably, the subject of the best diet is filled with controversy.

## Commercial vs. Home-prepared Diets

The first point of contention is whether dogs are better off being fed commercially prepared diets or home-prepared diets. The answer is not simple.

Critics of commercial foods point out that these foods are highly processed, do not resemble a dog's natural diet, are not fresh, and may use ingredients unfit for human consumption. Proponents of commercial foods point out that these diets

*Empty bowl syndrome...*

have been constantly adjusted and tested on generations of dogs to provide optimal nutrition, and that premium-grade foods contain human-quality ingredients.

Raw food diets have gained a lot of attention and supporters. These diets advocate more natural feeding by giving dogs whole raw animal carcasses, particularly chicken, which the dog eats, bones and all. Proponents point out that such diets are more like the natural diet of ancestral dogs, and claim good health, clean teeth, and economical food bills. Controlled studies on the safety and efficacy of such diets have yet to be published.

Detractors point out that, while the raw diet may be closer to what wolves eat, dogs are no longer wolves and haven't lived off the land for thousands of generations. In addition, many people have over-simplified these diets and commonly feed an exclusive diet of chicken wings, which is neither natural nor balanced. Critics also worry that raw foods from processing plants may pose the threat of salmonella and

*E. coli*. Although dogs are more resistant to these illnesses than people, they are not immune to them. If raw food is fed it should only be fresh and locally processed.

A third, and perhaps the best, alternative is to cook home-made diets according to recipes devised by canine nutritionists. Such diets provide a variety of nutrients in fresh foods according to accepted nutrition standards for dogs, but they are more labor-intensive than other choices. Ask your veterinarian to suggest a source for home-prepared menus.

It is a tribute to the dog's general hardiness that most dogs survive

*GOLD NUGGET*

**Dog Taste**
Dogs have most of the same taste receptors that we do, including similar sugar receptors, which explains why many have a sweet tooth. But their perception of artificial sweeteners is not like ours, and they seem to taste bitter to them. Research has shown that dogs, in general, prefer meat—not exactly earthshaking news—and while there are many individual differences, the average dog prefers beef, pork, lamb, chicken, and horsemeat, in that order.

under any of these feeding schemes, but for your dog to blossom, you may have to do some experimenting and understand some basics of canine nutrition.

# Evaluating Commercial Foods

If you choose to feed commercial food, feed a high-quality food from a name-brand company that states it meets the recommended minimal nutrient levels for dogs set by the Association of American Feed Control Officials (AAFCO) and has been tested through actual feeding trials. Always strive to buy and use only the freshest food available. Dry food loses nutrients as it sits, and the fat content can become rancid.

*Fresh foods, even fruits and vegetables, should be a part of your dog's diet. Introduce your pup to the food you want him to enjoy as an adult by giving them as treats.*

Dogs are omnivorous, meaning their nutritional needs can best be met by a diet derived from both animals and plants. These nutrients are commercially available in several forms. Dry food, containing about 10 percent moisture, is the most popular, economical, and healthy, but least enticing form of dog food. Semimoist food, with about 30 percent moisture, contains high levels of sugar used as preservatives. It is tasty, convenient, and very handy for traveling, but is not an optimal nutritional choice as a regular diet.

Canned food has a high moisture content—about 75 percent—which helps to make it tasty, but it also makes it comparatively expensive, since you're in essence buying water.

# Canine Nutrition

A good rule of thumb is that three or four of the first six ingredients of a dog food should be animal-derived. These tend to be tastier and more highly digestible than plant-based

---

*G O L D    N U G G E T*

## Definitions of Commercial Dog Food Ingredients

**Meat:** Mammal flesh including muscle, skin, heart, esophagus, and tongue.

**Meat by-products:** Cleaned mammal organs including kidneys, stomach, intestines, brain, spleen, lungs, and liver, plus blood, bone, and fatty tissue.

**Meat- and bonemeal:** Product rendered from processed meat and meat products, not including blood.

**Poultry by-products:** Cleaned poultry organs, plus feet and heads.

**Poultry by-products meal:** Product rendered from processed poultry by-products.

**Fishmeal:** Dried ground fish.

**Beef tallow:** Fat.

**Soybean meal:** By-product of soybean oil.

**Cornmeal:** Ground whole corn kernels.

**Corn gluten meal:** Dried residue after the removal of bran, germ, and starch from corn.

**Brewer's rice:** Fragmented rice kernels separated from milled rice.

**Cereal food fines:** Small particles of human breakfast cereals.

**Beet pulp:** Dried residue from sugar beets, added for fiber.

**Peanut hulls:** Ground peanut shells, added for fiber.

**BHA, BHT, ethoxyquin, sodium nitrate, tocopherols (vitamins C and E):** Preservatives; of these, the tocopherols are generally considered to present the least health risks but also have the shortest shelf life.

ingredients; more highly digestible foods generally mean less stool volume and fewer gas problems.

When comparing food labels, keep in mind that differences in

moisture content make it difficult to make direct comparisons between the guaranteed analyses in different forms of food, unless you first do some calculations to equate the percentage of dry matter food. The components that vary most from one brand to another are protein and fat percentages.

**Protein:** Protein provides the necessary building blocks for growth and maintenance of bones, muscle, and coat, and in the production of infection-fighting antibodies. The quality of protein is as important as its quantity. Meat-derived protein is higher quality and more highly digestible than plant-derived protein. This means that two foods with identical protein percentages can differ in the nutritional level of protein according to the protein's source.

Most Goldens will do fine on regular adult foods that have protein levels of about 20 to 22 percent (dry food percentage). Stressed, highly active, or underweight dogs should be fed higher protein levels. Puppies, as well as pregnant and nursing mothers, need particularly high protein and somewhat higher fat levels in their diets, such as the levels found in puppy foods. It was formerly thought that older dogs should be fed low-protein diets in order to avoid kidney problems, but it's now known that high-protein diets do not cause kidney failure. In fact, high-quality protein is essential to dogs with compromised kidney function. Such dogs should have reduced phosphorus levels, however, and

> ## GOLD NUGGET
>
> ### Feeding and Hip Dysplasia
>
> It's human nature to want to feed your growing puppy the best food possible, and most people would consider the best food to be the one highest in protein and calories to help puppies grow. Recent studies have shown that such diets are not a good idea for large breeds, and in particular, breeds that are prone to develop hip dysplasia. The rapid growth and weight gain that these diets provide apparently places stress on the dog's joints. Although it was originally thought that high-protein diets caused the problem, it's now believed that high-calorie diets are the main culprits. High-calorie diets don't cause dysplasia, but they increase the probability that a dog genetically predisposed to hip dysplasia will develop it. The current recommendation is to switch from puppy food to a food with fewer calories at about four or five months of age. Most important is that you don't let your pup get overweight. A lower-calorie diet will result in slower growth rate, but with no decrease in ultimate size.

*The more active Golden will need more fuel.*

there are special diets available that satisfy these requirements.

**Fat:** Fat is the calorie-rich component of foods, and most dogs prefer the taste of foods with higher fat content. Fat is necessary to good health, aiding in the transport of important vitamins and providing energy. Dogs deficient in fat, usually from diets containing less than 5 percent dry matter fat, may have sparse, dry coats and scaly skin. Excessive fat intake can cause obesity and appetite reduction, creating a deficiency in other nutrients. Working dogs usually need a high-fat diet to meet their high energy requirements. Obese dogs or dogs with heart problems, pancreatitis, or diarrhea should be fed a low-fat food.

**Carbohydrates:** Carbohydrates are a fairly inexpensive source of nutrition and make up a large part of most commercial dog foods. Excessive amounts of carbohydrates in the diet can cause decreased performance, diarrhea, and flatulence. Carbohydrates in most dog foods are primarily plant-derived. Many carbohydrates are poorly utilized by the dog's digestive system. Those derived from rice are best utilized, those from potato and corn, far less so, and wheat, oat, and beans, even less. Cooking increases the nutrient availability.

**Fiber:** Fiber in dog food varies considerably. Better-quality fiber sources include beet pulp and rice bran, but even these should provide a small percentage of a food's ingredients. Too much fiber interferes with digestion and can cause diarrhea or larger stool volume. Weight-reducing

## GOLD NUGGET

### Water

Water is essential for your dog's health and comfort. Don't just keep your dog's water bowl full by topping it up every day, as this allows algae to form along the sides of the bowl, and gives bacteria an opportunity to multiply. Empty, scrub, and refill the water bowl daily.

diets often include larger amounts of fiber, so the dog will feel fuller and to prevent digestibility of some of the other nutrients.

**Note:** A dog's optimal level of each nutrient will change according to its age, energy requirements, and state of health. Prescription commercial diets and recipes for home-prepared diets are available for dogs with various illnesses or needs.

# Feeding and Weight

It's seldom a good idea to let a Golden self-feed by leaving food available at all times. Food that is wet can spoil, and many Goldens overindulge. It's usually better to feed your dog on a schedule. Adult dogs can be fed once a day, but it is better to feed smaller meals twice a day. Very young puppies should be fed three or four times a day, on a regular schedule. Feed them as much as they care to eat in about 15 minutes. From the age of three to six months, pups should be fed three times daily, and after that, twice daily. By feeding discrete meals, you can get a good idea if your dog is eating as it should be.

You should also monitor the amount you feed by your dog's weight. All dogs have different metabolisms, so each dog's diet must be adjusted accordingly.

## Weight-reduction Diets

The Golden Retriever is an athlete, and should have a lean, muscular body. The ribs should be easily felt through a layer of muscle, and there should be no roll of fat over the withers or rump. Obesity predisposes dogs to joint injuries and heart problems and makes many preexisting problems worse.

Overweight Goldens should be fed a lower-calorie diet. The role of high fiber in reducing diets is controversial; recent studies suggest it does not provide the lowered hunger perception it was once thought to. Commercially available diet foods supply about 15 percent fewer calories per pound and are preferable to the alternative of simply feeding less of a fattening food. Home-prepared diets are available that are both tasty and less fattening.

Many people find that one of the many pleasures of dog ownership is sharing a special treat with their pet, but you can substitute a low-calorie alternative such as rice cakes or carrots. Keep your dog out of the kitchen or dining area at food preparation times and mealtimes. Schedule a walk immediately following your dinner to get your dog's mind off your leftovers; it will be good for both of you.

If your dog continues to be overweight, seek your veterinarian's opinion. In fact, your dog should be checked before embarking on any serious weight reduction effort. Heart disease and some endocrine disorders, such as hypothyroidism or Cushing's disease, or the early stages of diabetes, can cause the appearance of obesity and should be ruled out or treated. A dog in which only the stomach is enlarged, without fat around the shoulders or rump, is especially suspect and should be examined by a veterinarian. However, most fat Goldens are simply fat!

## Weight-gaining Diets

It's more unusual to see a skinny Golden. A dog that loses weight rapidly or steadily for no apparent reason should be seen by a veterinarian. Several diseases, including cancer, can cause wasting.

A few dogs just don't gain weight well, and some are just picky eaters. Underweight dogs may gain weight with puppy food; add water, milk, bouillon, ground beef, or canned food, and heat slightly to increase aroma and palatability. Milk will cause many dogs to have diarrhea, so try only a little bit at first. Of course, once you start this, you know you're making your picky eater pickier!

A sick or recuperating dog may have to be coaxed into eating. Cat

*The way to a Golden's heart is through his stomach, and every Golden learns early that the way to his stomach is through your soft heart.*

food and meat baby food are both relished by dogs and may entice a dog without an appetite to eat. Or try cooking chicken breasts or other meat, but ask your veterinarian first.

# Eating-related Disorders

Just as people do, dogs can get sick to their stomachs from eating the wrong things (see page 47 for signs of poisoning). Some other types of food-related illnesses are equally serious but often go unrecognized until it's too late.

### Pancreatitis

Pancreatitis (inflammation of the pancreas) is more common in older or middle-aged dogs, especially overweight ones. It is often precipitated by a high-fat meal, and is the most common illness associated with Thanksgiving and Christmas. Symptoms include lack of appetite, lethargy, and signs of abdominal discomfort—such as standing with front legs down on the ground as in a bowing position—and possibly vomiting, diarrhea, and even shock or death. Although most dogs can eat a high-fat meal without a problem, once a dog develops pancreatitis, a high-fat meal often precipitates subsequent episodes.

### Food Allergies

Symptoms of food allergies range from diarrhea to itchy skin and ears. If you suspect your dog has a food allergy, consult your veterinarian about an elimination diet, in which you start with a bland diet consisting of ingredients your dog has never eaten before. Lamb and rice foods used to be vigorously promoted as hypoallergenic, but because a dog is now likely to have eaten lamb previously, that is no longer true. Your veterinarian can suggest sources of protein, such as venison, duck, or rabbit, which your dog will probably not have eaten previously. You may have to keep the dog on this diet for at least a month, withholding treats, pills, and even toys that might be creating an allergic response. If the symptoms go away, then ingredients are added back to the diet gradually, or a novel commercial diet is tried. It may take a lot of experimentation, but a healthy and happy dog will be well worth it.

### Gastric Dilatation Volvulus (GDV)

Commonly called *bloat*, GDV is a life-threatening emergency in which gas and fluid become trapped in the stomach. It is most common in large, deep-chested breeds, especially those with narrow bodies and tucked-up abdomens. In the largest study of GDV to date, several factors affecting GDV emerged. Dogs that are underweight, fearful, excitable, and fast eaters, and that eat only one meal a day are more likely to bloat. Dogs with happy, stable temperaments, and dogs that eat some canned food and table scraps are less likely to bloat. The dogs at greatest risk are those with a close relative that had GDV, suggesting a genetic component. The commonly suggested methods used to avoid bloat—restricting water and exercise before and after eating, raising the food bowl, and administering anti-gas medication—were not found to lower the incidence of GDV.

To be on the safe side, avoid other suspected risk factors, which means you should:
• feed several small meals instead of one large meal.
• include some canned food or table scraps.
• not allow the dog to gulp food.
• not allow your dog to be stressed around its mealtime.
• premoisten food, especially foods that expand when moistened.

## Pica and Copraphagia

Dogs can eat a variety of strange things. Pica, the ingestion of non-

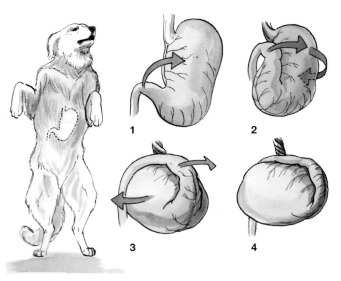

*The progression of gastric dilation.*

food items, such as wood, fabric, or soil, can be a problem in some dogs. Talk to your veterinarian about possible health problems that could contribute to these specific hungers,

---

### GOLD NUGGET

### GDV Is an Emergency!

Symptoms of GDV include distention of the abdomen, unproductive attempts to vomit, excessive salivation, and restlessness. A dog with these symptoms needs to be taken to the emergency clinic immediately—not tomorrow, not even an hour from now. No home treatment is possible. The veterinarian will try to pass a tube into the stomach so gases can escape, but often this isn't possible because the stomach has twisted and rotated on its axis. The rotation of the stomach cuts off the blood supply to the stomach wall, which will subsequently kill the dog if surgery isn't performed very quickly. Other organs may also be compromised. During surgery, the veterinarian should tack the stomach in place to prevent future rotation. Dogs that bloat once will often continue to do so without this tacking procedure.

*Goldens have an "oral fixation," but sometimes they carry it too far and eat foreign objects.*

GOLD NUGGET

**Varying the Diet**

Most dogs, unless they've been raised on only one food, prefer a varied menu, and varying a dog's diet can offer some insurance that he's getting proper nutrition by providing a wide range of ingredients. In fact, dogs tend to prefer a new food, but then tire of it within a few days; however, many dogs develop diarrhea at abrupt changes in diet, so you must be sure to change foods gradually with these dogs.

and about possible problems that could result from eating these items.

The most common and disturbing nonfood item eaten by dogs is feces. This habit, called coprophagia, has been blamed on boredom, stress, hunger, poor nutrition, and excessively rich nutrition, but none of these explanations has proved to be completely satisfactory. Food additives are available that make the stool less savory to the dog, and you can also try adding hot pepper to it, but a determined dog will not be deterred and the best cure is immediate removal of all feces. Many puppies experiment with stool eating but grow out of it.

## Vomiting

Consult your veterinarian immediately if your dog vomits a foul substance resembling fecal matter, indicating a blockage in the intestinal tract, blood (partially digested blood resembles coffee grounds), or if there is projectile or repeated vomiting. Repeated vomiting—more than three or four bouts, or always after eating or drinking in the course of a day—can result in dehydration, so if your dog can't hold anything down for a prolonged period, he may have to be given intravenous fluids. Other common causes of vomiting:

• Overeating, especially when followed by playing.

• Regurgitation immediately after meals, which can indicate an esophageal obstruction.

• Repeated vomiting, which can result from spoiled food, indigestible objects, or a stomach illness.

• Sporadic vomiting with poor appetite and generally poor condition, which could indicate internal parasites or a more serious disease.

## Diarrhea

Diarrhea can result from excitement, nervousness, a change in diet or water, sensitivity to certain foods, overeating, intestinal parasites, viral or bacterial infections, or ingestion of toxic substances. Its consistency,

*The Working retriever reflects the Golden at its best: athletic, intelligent, courageous, and attentive—a true outdoor companion.*

# GOLD NUGGET

## Commonly Ingested Poisons

- Ethylene glycol-based antifreeze causes kidney failure; the prognosis is poor once symptoms appear. The dog must have veterinary treatment within two to four hours of ingestion of even tiny amounts if his life is to be saved.
- Warfarin-based rodent poisons contain anticoagulants that cause uncontrolled internal bleeding; the prognosis ranges from good, if caught soon after ingestion, to poor, if several days have elapsed.
- Cholecalciferol-based rodent poisons deposit calcium in the blood vessels, causing kidney failure and other problems; the prognosis is poor, even from eating small amounts.
- Strychnine-based squirrel and bird poisons, usually administered as birdseed with a blue coating of strychnine, can cause seizures, hyperreactivity to noise, and rigid muscles. The prognosis is poor.
- Metaldehyde-based snail and slug poisons cause anxiety, unsteadiness, tremors, coma, and death; the prognosis is fair.
- Arsenic-based insect poisons, weed killers, and wood preservatives cause vomiting, diarrhea, and weakness, progressing to kidney failure, coma, and death; the prognosis is poor if symptoms have already started.
- Organophosphate-based flea and tick poisons and dewormers, in overdose quantities, can cause vomiting, muscle tremors, pupil constriction, diarrhea, excitability, difficulty breathing, and death. The prognosis varies but can be poor.
- Theobromine, found in chocolate, can cause vomiting, diarrhea, restlessness, fever, seizures, coma, and death; toxic dose for dogs is 50 mg/lb. Dark chocolate contains over 400 mg/oz., so a 5-ounce (140-g) candy bar can be life-threatening to a 40-pound (18-kg) dog.
- Lead, found in paint, golf ball coatings, linoleum, and even newsprint, causes abnormal behavior, unsteadiness, seizures, loss of appetite, vomiting, diarrhea, and blindness; the prognosis is usually good.
- Zinc, found in pennies, zinc oxide skin cream, calamine lotion, fertilizers, and shampoos, causes breakdown of red blood cells. Symptoms include decreased appetite, vomiting, diarrhea, depression, pale gums, and brown urine; the prognosis is variable.
- Iron-based rose fertilizers can cause kidney and liver failure; toxic dose is 1 teaspoon of 5 percent concentration per 20-pound (9-kg) dog. The prognosis is variable depending upon dosage and treatment delay.

color, and contents, such as, parasites, blood, mucus, or foreign objects, are all clues to the severity and possible causes of your dog's problem.

Diarrhea with vomiting, fever, or other signs of toxicity, or diarrhea that lasts for more than a day or that is bloody should not be allowed to continue without seeking veterinary advice. You can treat mild diarrhea by withholding or severely restricting food and water for 24 hours. You can give the dog ice cubes to satisfy his thirst. Administer human antidiarrhea medication in the same weight dosage as recommended for humans only if advised to do so by your veterinarian. Feed a bland diet consisting of rice, tapioca, or cooked macaroni, along with cottage cheese or tofu for protein. Note that dogs with some concurrent illnesses may not be candidates for food or water restriction.

## Poisoning

Signs of poisoning commonly include vomiting, convulsions, staggering, and collapse. If in doubt about whether poison was ingested, call the veterinarian anyway.

If the dog has ingested the poison within the past two hours, and is not severely depressed, convulsing, or comatose, you may be advised to induce vomiting, unless the poison was an acid, alkali, petroleum product, solvent, cleaner, or tranquilizer. You can do this by giving hydrogen peroxide, mixed 1:1 with water, saltwater, or dry mustard and water.

In other cases you may be advised to dilute the poison by giving milk, vegetable oil, or egg whites. Activated charcoal can adsorb many toxins. Baking soda or milk of magnesia can be given for ingested acids, and vinegar or lemon juice for ingested alkalis.

## Chapter Five
# The Midas Touch

Grooming is not only important for the sake of beauty; it also can prevent serious health problems. Just as with people, good grooming involves more than an occasional brushing of the hair. Keeping the nails, teeth, eyes, and ears well groomed is just as, if not more, important.

## Hair Care

Part of the glory of a Golden Retriever is its golden coat. The best way to get a good coat is to grow it from the inside, and that means proper nutrition. You can help that coat stay healthy by caring for it on the outside, and that means brushing and washing.

### Brushing

Brushing is blissful for most Goldens, as long as it doesn't involve pulling on tangles. If you wait too long to get started or between sessions, the coat can become matted and grooming will be a battle neither of you looks forward to. An adult

*Good grooming will make your Golden glow.*

Golden will need brushing one to three times a week, and even more during shedding season. Putting it off will only cause you more work.

Mist the coat ever so slightly with water before starting; brushing a dry coat can result in hair breakage. Then use a pin brush to get out most of the tangles. Be sure you get all the layers down to the skin. Start at the bottom of the dog and work up, lifting the coat and brushing it layer by layer in thicker areas.

If you come across a tangle or small mat, try picking it apart with the end of the comb, your fingers, or a mat rake. Big mats can be cut into strips with blunt-nosed scissors; slip a comb between the mat and the skin to make sure you don't cut the dog. Then try to work with the smaller mats.

The next step will depend on your plans for your dog and its state of shedding. Nothing pulls out dead and shedding hair like a slicker brush or a shedding rake. Unfortunately, from a show grooming point of view, they are also great at removing living hair. Use these if you want to get rid of as much hair as possible, but use them sparingly if

GOLD NUGGET

**Grooming Equipment**
For a top quality job you will need:
- Wide-toothed comb
- Narrow-toothed comb
- Slicker brush
- Bristle brush
- Pin brush
- Blunt-nosed scissors
- Thinning scissors
- Stripping knife
- Rake
- Misting spray bottle

you are trying to cultivate a show coat or preserve a coat just starting to shed.

Use a comb on the feathers of the forelegs, chest, tail, and britches, and to search for overlooked tangles on the rest of the dog. A bristle brush can be used to remove dirt and distribute oils, but if the air is dry it can cause the coat to have static electricity.

### Bathing

You will save yourself work in the long run by brushing your Golden before bathing. Wetting tangled hairs causes them to bunch up and mat even more tightly. Removing dead hair also helps water and shampoo penetrate down to the skin, and with the Golden's dense, water-repellent coat, you need all the help you can get.

Your choice of shampoo will depend on your dog's coat and your intentions for your dog. For the best results, use a good shampoo formulated specifically for dogs. Even the fanciest human shampoos aren't as good as these, because dogs and human hair have different pH values and therefore need different shampoos. Dog skin has a pH of 7.5, while human skin has a pH of 5.5; bathing in a shampoo formulated for the pH of human skin can lead to scaling and irritation. It's not that human shampoo will do dire things to your dog if you use it, it's just that it won't give you as good a result as dog shampoo and, if your dog has dry skin or other skin and coat problems, it could make them worse. In fact, if you're on a budget and your dog has healthy skin and coat, a mild liquid dishwashing detergent can actually give good results.

*Grooming should be a pleasurable bonding experience for both dog and people.*

If you want top-class results you need to use a top-class dog shampoo that's right for your dog. If your dog's coat is too limp, you can get one with a texturizer; if it's too full, you can get one with conditioner; if it's too oily, you can get one that cuts oil better. Some shampoos have brighteners and some have ingredients that claim to bring out the gold coloration. Other shampoos are available from your veterinarian and are effective for various skin problems. Oatmeal-based antipruritics can help sooth itchy skin, moisturizing shampoos can help dry skin, antiseborrheic shampoos can help with excessive greasy scaling and dandruff, and antimicrobials can help damaged skin. No dog owner should be without one of the dog shampoos that requires no water or rinsing. These are wonderful for puppies, spot baths, and emergencies.

If you use your own tub for dog bathing, place a nonskid mat in the bottom of it and help your dog in and out so he doesn't slip. A hand-held sprayer is essential for indoor bathing. Remember to use water that you would be comfortable using for your own shower. Warm water tends to open the hair follicles and helps loosen dead hair. Keep one hand under the spray so you can monitor the water temperature.

**1.** Start by wetting down the dog to the skin, leaving the head for last. Be sure the water isn't just running off the top of the dog. You need to soak the undercoat down to the skin.

**2.** Mix the shampoo with water first. Use a big sponge to apply it and then use your hands to work up a moderate lather.

**3.** Rinsing is a crucial step; shampoo remaining in the coat can cause dryness and itchiness. Begin rinsing from the front and top of the dog and work backwards and rearwards. To keep your dog from shaking, keep one hand clenched around the base of one ear.

**4.** Most Goldens don't require a cream rinse, but you can add a small amount if you like. A cream rinse will tend to make the hair lie flatter but may make it too soft and silky.

**Drying:** Don't let your dog outside on a chilly day when still wet from a bath. You have removed the oils from the coat and saturated your dog down to the skin, so he is far wetter than he would ever get by going swimming and thus more likely to become chilled. Some people believe allowing a wet dog to become chilled can cause "cold tail" (see page 73).

Once the Golden's thick undercoat gets soaked, it can take a long time to dry. Blow-drying is essential

---

## GOLD NUGGET

### Shampoos and Fleas
Most shampoos, even people shampoos, will kill fleas, but none, including flea shampoos, has any residual killing action on fleas.

GOLD NUGGET

**Water Dogs**
Goldens that swim a lot should be dried whenever possible. A coat that remains wet much of the time is more apt to develop skin problems.

**1.** Start at the top and front of the dog, but behind the head. Be careful: The high force of the air can damage the eyes, ears, and other sensitive areas.

**2.** Hold the nozzle close to the dog and blow directly onto the hair so that it parts the hair down to the skin, blowing off water in all directions.

**3.** Once your dog is partially dry, he will probably look as though he's just stepped out of a cyclone—and he has, in a way. Use a pin brush to make the hair lie in the direction it grows, which is generally toward the rear and down. Now use the forced air to encourage the hair to lie close to the body as it dries by blowing it in the direction it grows, this time trying not to allow the hair to fly around crazily. To do this you must

if you want a show-dog finish to your grooming. You can use an inexpensive human hair blow dryer, but they dry with heat, which can damage the hair and be uncomfortable on the dog's skin unless you're careful. A better, but more expensive, dryer is a forced-air dryer, which blows cool air at high pressure. Rather than relying upon evaporation, it literally blows the water off the dog's coat.

*Beware the wet dog shake!*

*Dogs that spend a lot of time wet are more susceptible to skin and coat problems.*

direct the air so that it flows in the direction of hair growth. You can also use a pin brush to help direct the hair while drying. The long feathering of the tail, chest, britches, and forelegs is brushed in the correct direction while being blown dry.

**4.** If you stop drying too soon, the dog's damp coat will dent and wrinkle when he lies down, ruining all your hard work. If that happens, sprinkle the affected area with water and blow it dry again.

## Trimming

The first rule of trimming a Golden is that less is best! This is a natural breed that should never be sculpted into a perfect silhouette. A Golden with a proper coat will not have excessively long hair; still, some straggling hairs can be cut off. If your dog has extremely long feathering you may wish to shorten it so that leaves and sticks are less likely to get caught in it, but it's so pretty you won't want to do too much. If you trim before rather than after bathing, you can better achieve a natural look.

If you are grooming for the show ring you will need to do some additional thinning or trimming. Sometimes the hair grows too thick in some areas, particularly over the withers, giving the illusion of a lumpy topline. You can carefully use a stripping knife to remove some of the excess coat, but on some dogs, the remaining hair will be a lighter color—this is not something to try the night before the show. You can also use the stripping knife or thinning shears to smooth the transition from the neck into the shoulder area. The ruff should be left intact.

The tail may be trimmed slightly so that it tapers near the end, but not so much as is characteristically seen on setters.

**1.** Start by holding the tail straight out by the hair at the tail tip. Twist the hair at the tip, then cut it to a length of about ¾ of an inch (19 mm). At the proper length, the hair tip should reach just to the point of hock when the tail hangs straight down.

**2.** Still holding the tail straight out, use thinning shears to taper the hair on the underside so it meets the hair at the tip. The tail should have a rounded, yet tapered, appearance.

### Ear Grooming

Ear grooming looks deceptively simple. Most Goldens have a lot of fluffies under their ear, so start there.

**1.** Use a stripping comb to remove some of the thick undercoat, and continue until the hair is lying relatively flat. In extra fluffy cases, you may have to use thinning shears (but sparingly!) as well. Repeat this procedure with the stripping comb, and, if necessary, the thinning shears, behind the ears.

**2.** The outer earflaps are more critical. Your goal is to have them covered fairly uniformly with close-lying hair. You will usually need to comb the hair backwards and thin ever so carefully with the thinning shears, cutting with the shears held in line with the length, rather than width, of the ear.

**3.** Finally, use the thinning shears to even up the hair along the ear's edges—but not too evenly.

### Feet and Pasterns

Tidy the hair around the feet and pasterns. This is even a good idea for pet dogs, since hairy feet carry more dirt into your house.

**1.** Use small blunt-tipped scissors to trim any long hair growing between the pads beneath the foot so that it is even with the pads.

**2.** Trim along the outer edge of the foot so that no hair touches the

*The well-groomed Golden is happier and healthier—and maybe just a little bit conceited!*

ground and the whole foot has an even, rounded, appearance.

**3.** Use a flea comb or slicker brush against the direction of hair growth so the short hair on top of the toes is sticking out, then use the thinning shears, cutting in line with each toe, to remove the extra hairs. Comb the hair back down.

**4.** Trim the hair behind the pastern so that it follows the heel of the back of the foot pad, and smooth and neaten the longer hairs from the stop pad down.

If possible, get an experienced Golden groomer to show you how to bring out the best in your particular dog. Don't put off your first attempt at show grooming until right before the show. Even then, you might want to do your first trims on the right side of the dog (the side the judge doesn't see much)—just in case you mess it up.

Finally, don't do too perfect a job. Goldens should look like they just stepped out of the field rather than the beauty parlor. Always remember: When in doubt, don't cut it out!

# Skin Problems

Skin problems make up most of the "non-well" cases a veterinarian sees every day. Problems can result from parasites, allergies, bacteria, fungus, endocrine disorders, and a long list of other possible causes.

### Fleas

Recent advances have finally put dog owners on the winning side in the fight against fleas. In any but the mildest of infestations, the new products available are well worth their initial higher purchase price. It's a lot cheaper to put an expensive product on your dog once every three months than to reapply a cheap one every day.

Always read the ingredients. You may think you're getting a deal with a less expensive product that is applied the same and boasts of the same results as one of the more expensive products, but you're not getting a deal if it doesn't contain the right ingredients. Some of the major ingredients in the newer products are:

• Imidacloprid (for example, Advantage), a liquid applied once a month on the animal's back. It gradually distributes itself over the entire skin surface, kills at least 98 percent of

---

*G O L D   N U G G E T*

**Thinning and Stripping**

Anytime you use thinning shears, you should first comb the hair against the direction of growth so it is sticking out before you start cutting. This way, when you comb the hair back down, you are less likely to see teeth marks from the shears. The thinning shears can be used to remove excessive bulk of hair, but must also be used with great care. Stripping knives can also be handy for pulling out dead undercoat on shorter-haired areas.

GOLD NUGGET

**Fleas and Tapeworms**

Tapeworms look like moving white flat worms when fresh, or like rice grains, usually around the dog's anus, when dried out. Although they are one of the least debilitating of all the worms, their segments can produce anal itching. Because tapeworms are in the cestode family, they are not affected by the same kinds of dewormers and preventives as the other common worms, which are in the nematode family. The only preventive is to diligently rid your Golden of fleas, because fleas transmit the most common tapeworm (*Dipylidium*) to dogs.

the fleas on the animal within 24 hours, and will continue to kill fleas for a month. It can withstand water, but not repeated swimming or bathing.

• Fipronil (for example, Frontline), which comes as either a spray that you must apply all over the dog's body, or as a self-distributing liquid applied only on the dog's back. Once applied, fipronil collects in the hair follicles and then wicks out over time. It is thus resistant to being washed off and can kill fleas for up to three months on dogs. It is also effective on ticks for a shorter period.

• Lufenuron (for example, Program), given as a pill once a month. Fleas that bite the dog and ingest the lufenuron in the dog's system are rendered sterile. It is extremely safe. All animals in the environment must be treated in order for the regimen to be effective, however.

Traditional flea-control products are either less effective or less safe than these newer products. The permethrins and pyrethrins are safe, but have virtually no residual action. The large family of cholinesterase inhibitors (Dursban, Diazinon, malathion, Sevin, Carbaryl, Pro-Spot, Spotton) last a little longer, but have been known to kill dogs when overused, used in combination with cholinesterase inhibiting yard products, or with cholinesterase inhibiting dewormers. Ultrasonic flea-repelling collars have been shown to be both ineffective on fleas and irritating to dogs, and, contrary to some old wives' tales, feeding dogs brewer's yeast or garlic will not get rid of fleas.

### Ticks

Two newer products for tick control are amitraz collars (tick collars) and fipronil spray or liquid. Neither will keep ticks totally off your dog, but they may discourage them from staying or implanting. Even with these precautions you should still use your hands to feel for ticks in your dogs whenever you are in a potential tick-infested area.

Ticks can be found anywhere on the dog, but most often burrow around the ears, neck, chest, and between the toes.

**To remove a tick:** Use a tissue or tweezers, since some diseases, such as Lyme disease, can be transmitted to humans. Grasp the tick as close to the skin as possible, and pull slowly and steadily, trying not to leave the head in the dog. Don't squeeze the tick, as this can inject its contents into the dog. Clean the site with alcohol. Often, a bump will remain after the tick is removed, even if you got the head. It will go away with time.

## Mites

Mites are tiny organisms that are in the tick and spider family. Chemicals that are effective on fleas have no effect on mites. Of the many types of mites, only a few cause problems in dogs.

**Sarcoptic mange** is contagious and causes intense itching, often characterized by scaling of the ear tips, and small bumps and crusts of other affected areas. Most of the lesions are found on the ear tips, abdomen, elbows, and hocks. Treatment requires repeated shampoos or dips of not only the affected dog, but other household pets that are in contact with the infected dog. It is highly contagious, even to humans, and spread by direct contact. Skin scrapings may reveal the responsible *Sarcoptes scabiei* mite. The presence of just one mite lends a definite diagnosis, but the absence of mites doesn't mean they aren't present.

**Demodectic mange** is not contagious and is not usually itchy. Most cases of demodectic mange appear in puppies, and most consist of only a few patches that often go away by themselves. This localized variety is

GOLD NUGGET

**Ticks and Ehrlichiosis**

Ehrlichiosis is an under-diagnosed yet potentially fatal disease spread by ticks that parasitizes white blood cells and cripples the immune system. Symptoms may include lack of energy, a dull coat, occasional vomiting, occasional loss of appetite, coughing, arthritis, muscle wasting, seizures, spontaneous bleeding, anemia, or a host of other nonspecific signs. Aside from a fever in the initial phases of the disease, dogs may not exhibit definite signs of illness; they may just not seem "quite right." Definitive diagnosis is made by getting a blood titer and testing for all strains of ehrlichia. It can be treated effectively if caught early.

not considered hereditary. In some cases, it begins as a diffuse moth-eaten appearance, particularly around the lips and eyes or on the front legs, or the dog has many localized spots. These cases tend to get worse until the dog has generalized demodectic mange. Demodectic mange affecting the feet is also common, and can be extremely resistant to treatment. Aggressive treatment using repeated amitraz insecticidal dips is needed for generalized demodicosis, but is not suggested for localized. The hair should be clipped to allow the dips to penetrate to the skin more easily. Benzoyl peroxide

GOLD NUGGET

## Mosquitoes and Heartworm

Wherever mosquitoes are present, dogs should be on heartworm prevention. Monthly preventives don't stay in the dog's system for a month, but instead, act on a particular stage in the heartworm's development. Giving the drug each month prevents any heartworms from ever maturing.

The most common way of checking for heartworms is to check the blood for circulating microfilariae (the immature form of heartworms), but this method may fail to detect the presence of adult heartworms in as many as 20 percent of all tested dogs. More accurate is an "occult" heartworm test, which detects antigens to heartworms in the blood. With either test, the presence of heartworms will not be detectable until nearly seven months after infection. Heartworms are treatable in their early stages, but the treatment is expensive and not without risks, although a less risky treatment has recently become available. If untreated, heartworms can kill your pet.

shampoos have a follicular flushing action and should be used for both localized and generalized forms. A definite diagnosis with a skin scraping should be performed before

beginning treatment and before ending it. Because the *Demodex canis* mite is thought to be a normal inhabitant of the dog's hair follicles, the presence of occasional mites is not normally sufficient evidence to diagnose a dog with demodectic mange.

**Cheyletialla mites** are contagious and cause mild itchiness. They look like small white specks in the dog's hair near the skin. Many flea insecticides also kill these mites, but they are better treated by using special shampoos or dips.

Sarcoptic, demodectic, and cheyletialla mites have all been successfully eradicated with injections of ivermectin. This treatment is considered "off label" and should only be performed by a veterinarian in serious cases.

**Ear mites** are discussed on page 62.

### Skin Allergies

Many allergies can make your dog uncomfortable with relentless itching. Finding the source of the problem can be difficult, but some allergies are more common than others.

Allergens can be isolated with an intradermal skin test, in which small amounts of various allergen extracts are injected under the skin. The skin is then monitored for localized allergic reactions. Blood tests are also available and are less expensive, but they are not as comprehensive as skin testing. Either test should be performed by a veterinarian with training in the field of allergic skin diseases, as the results can be difficult to interpret.

**FAD:** Flea allergy dermatitis is the most common of all skin problems. When even one flea bites a susceptible dog, the flea's saliva causes an allergic reaction that results in intense itching, not only in the vicinity of the flea bite, but often all over the dog and especially on its rump, legs, and paws. The dog chews these areas and causes irritation leading to crusted bumps.

**Inhaled allergens:** Besides FAD, dogs can have allergic reactions to pollens or other inhaled allergens. Whereas human inhalant allergies usually result in respiratory symptoms, canine inhalant allergies usually result in itchy skin. The condition typically first appears in young dogs and gets progressively worse. The main sites of itching seem to be the face, ears, feet, forelegs, armpits, and abdomen. The dog rubs and chews these areas, traumatizing the skin and leading to secondary bacterial infections. Because the feet are so often affected, many people erroneously assume the dog is allergic to grass or dew. Although such contact allergies do exist, they are far less common than flea, inhalant, or food allergies. Food allergies are discussed on page 42.

**Hot spots:** A reddened, moist, itchy spot that suddenly appears is most likely a "hot spot" (pyotraumatic dermatitis), which arises from an itch-scratch-chew cycle resulting most commonly from fleas or allergies. Wash the area with an oat-

**GOLD NUGGET**

**Smelly Dogs**
Clean Goldens should not have a strong body odor. Doggy odor is not only offensive; it is unnatural. Check the mouth, ears, feet, anus, and genitals for infection. Impacted anal sacs can contribute to bad odor. Generalized bad odor can indicate a skin problem, such as seborrhea. Don't ignore bad odor, and don't make your dog take the blame for something you need to fix.

meal-based shampoo, blow it dry, and prevent the dog from further chewing. If possible, shave the area first. Several home remedies have been suggested, including the application of Listerine or Gold Bond powder, but these do not always work and severe cases should receive veterinary attention. Your veterinarian can also prescribe anti-inflammatory medication and, if needed, antibiotics. As a temporary measure, you can give an allergy pill (ask your veterinarian about dosage), which alleviates some itching and causes drowsiness, both of which should decrease chewing.

# Nail Care

Canine nails evolved to withstand traveling many miles every day. Unless your dog is a marathon runner, you're going to need to trim his nails regularly. The most common

GOLD NUGGET

**Skunk!**

In case of skunk spray: Mix one pint of 3 percent hydrogen peroxide, ⅔ cup baking soda, and one teaspoon of liquid soap or citrus-based dog shampoo with one gallon (3.8 L) of water. Use immediately. Wear gloves and sponge it on the dog. Leave it on the dog about five minutes, rinse, and repeat if needed. Caution: this solution may slightly bleach the coat.

problem associated with overly long nails occurs when the nail becomes snagged on a tree root or even a carpet loop, pulling the nail from its bed or dislocating the toe. In addition, overly long nails impact on the ground with every step, causing discomfort and eventually splayed feet and lameness. If dewclaws (the rudimentary "thumbs" on the wrists) are left untrimmed, they can get caught on things more easily and can be ripped out or actually loop around and grow into the dog's leg. You must prevent this by trimming your dog's nails every week or two.

It is easier to cut the nails by holding the foot backward, much as a horse's hoof is held when being shod. This way your Golden can't see what's going on, and you can see the bottom of the nail. Here you will see a solid core culminating in a hollowed nail. Cut the tip up to the core, but not beyond. On occasion,

you will slip up and cause the nail to bleed. Apply styptic powder to the nail to stop the bleeding. If this is not available, dip the nail in flour or hold it to a wet tea bag. And be more careful the next time!

# Ear Care

Unlike in humans, the dog's ear canal is made up of an initial long vertical segment that then abruptly angles to run horizontally toward the skull. This configuration provides a moist environment in which various ear infections can flourish. Earflaps that hang down, especially those with long hair around the ear canal, tend to block the aeration of the ear. Dogs that swim a lot are more likely to get water in their ears. The combination of moisture without aeration makes the ear prone to problems. Check your dog's ears regularly and don't allow moisture or debris to accumulate in them.

Ear problems can be difficult to cure once they have become established, so early veterinary attention is crucial. Signs of ear problems include inflammation, discharge, debris, foul odor, pain, scratching, shaking, tilting of the head, or circling to one side. Bacterial and yeast infections, ear mites or ticks, foreign bodies, inhalant allergies, seborrhea, or hypothyroidism are possible underlying problems. Because the ear canal is lined with skin, any skin disorder that affects the dog elsewhere can also strike its ears.

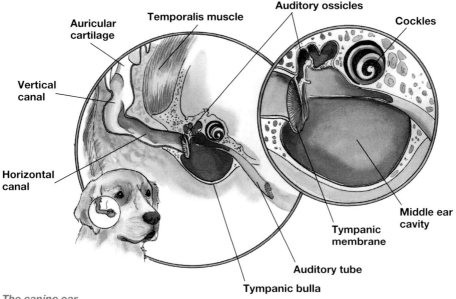

*The canine ear.*

Fox tails (see page 72) are a common cause of ear problems in dogs that spend time outdoors. Keep the ear lubricated with mineral oil, and seek veterinary treatment as soon as possible if there is a problem.

If your dog has ear debris but no signs of discomfort or itching, you can try cleaning the ear yourself, but be forewarned that overzealous cleaning can irritate the skin lining the ear canal. You can buy products to clean the ear or use a homemade mixture of one part alcohol to two parts white vinegar. Hold the ear near its base and quickly squeeze in the ear cleaner; the slower it drips, the more it will tickle.

Gently massage the liquid downward and squish it all around. Then stand back and let your dog shake it all out—be sure you're outdoors. If the ear has so much debris that repeated rinses don't clean it up promptly, you

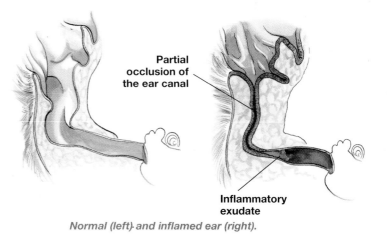

*Normal (left) and inflamed ear (right).*

have a problem that will need veterinary attention. If the ear is red, swollen, or painful, do not attempt to clean it yourself. Your dog may need to be sedated for cleaning, and may have a serious problem. Cleaning solutions will flush debris but will not kill mites or cure infections. Don't stick cotton swabs down in the ear canal, as they can irritate the skin and pack debris into the horizontal canal. Don't use powders, which can cake in the ear, or hydrogen peroxide, which can leave the ear moist.

**Ear mites:** Ear mites are primarily found in puppies or ill adults. An affected dog will scratch his ears, shake his head, and perhaps hold his head sideways. The ear mite's signature is a dark, dry, waxy buildup resembling coffee grounds in the ear canal, usually of both ears. Some-

times, the tiny mites can be seen with a magnifying glass if the material is placed on a dark background.

Separate a dog with ear mites from other pets and wash your hands after handling his ears. Ideally, every pet in a household should be treated. Your veterinarian can provide the best medication. Because ear mites are also found in the dog's fur all over his body, you should also treat the dog's fur with a pyrethrin-based shampoo or spray.

## Eye Care

Eye care should never be approached with a wait-and-see attitude. Take note of squinting, redness, itching, tearing, dullness, mucus discharge, or any change in pupil size or reactivity. Anytime your dog's pupils do not react to light, or when one eye reacts differently from another, take him to the veterinarian immediately. It could indicate a serious ocular or neurological problem.

**Discharge:** Squinting or tearing can be due to an irritated cornea or foreign body. Examine under the lids and flood the eye with saline solution, or use a moist cotton swab to remove any debris. A watery discharge without squinting can be a symptom of allergies or a tear drainage problem. A clogged tear drainage duct can cause the tears to drain onto the face rather than the normal drainage through the nose. Your veterinarian can diagnose a drainage problem with a simple test.

*Proper care of your Golden will help him experience the world with all of his senses at their fullest.*

A thick mucus discharge usually indicates a more serious problem, including conjunctivitis, lid irritation, or "dry eye" (keratoconjunctivitis sicca). These conditions should be treated by your veterinarian.

**Lens opacites:** As your Golden ages, it is natural that the lens of the eye becomes a little hazy. You will notice this as a slightly grayish appearance behind the pupils. If this occurs at a young age, however, or if the lens looks white or opaque, ask your veterinarian to check your dog for cataracts. In cataracts, the lens becomes so opaque that light can no longer reach the retina; as in humans, the lens can be surgically replaced with an artificial lens.

# Dental Care

Between four and seven months of age, Golden puppies will begin to shed their baby teeth and show off new permanent teeth. Often, deciduous (baby) teeth, especially the canines (fangs), are not shed, so that the permanent tooth grows in beside the baby tooth. If this condition persists after the permanent teeth are fully in, consult your veterinarian. Retained baby teeth can cause misalignment of adult teeth. Correct occlusion is important for good dental health. In a correct Golden bite, the top incisors should fit snugly in front of the bottom incisors, with the top canines just behind the bottom canines. If the bottom canines are behind or opposed to the top

**GOLD NUGGET**

**Other Eye Problems**
Several ocular disorders with hereditary causes are described on page 84.

canines, the bottom ones can be displaced inward and pierce the palate every time the mouth is closed.

Tooth plaque and tartar are not only unsightly, but contribute to bad breath and health problems. If not removed, plaque will attract bacteria and minerals, which will harden into tartar. Plaque can cause infections to form along the gum line, then spread rootward causing irreversible periodontal disease with tissue, bone, and tooth loss. The bacteria may also sometimes enter the bloodstream and cause infection in the kidneys and heart valves.

Dry food and hard dog biscuits, carrots, rawhide and dental chewies are only minimally helpful in removing plaque. Prescription dog food is available that will decrease tartar accumulation, but brushing your Golden's teeth (optimally daily) with a dog toothpaste (not human!) and brush is the best plaque remover. Most Goldens are surprisingly cooperative. Your dog's teeth may have to be cleaned under anesthesia as often as once a year if you do not brush them.

A well-groomed Golden feels better, looks better, and has a head start on a long and healthy life. You wouldn't want any less for him.

## Chapter Six

# Gold Medalist Medicine

Your Golden doesn't have to be a sports star to get a sports injury. Goldens play and work hard, and not surprisingly, they occasionally hurt themselves. Most Goldens are pretty tough and will recover with only rest. Some injuries need a little more attention, however, to prevent permanent damage and keep your Golden at the top of his game.

## The Five-minute Checkup

Even if you don't have a sports star, the best five minutes you can spend with your dog every week is performing a quick health check. You'll be getting to know how your dog looks when healthy, you'll get a head start on any problems, and your dog will think you just can't resist petting him all over. Check:

• mouth for red, bleeding, swollen or pale gums, loose teeth, ulcers of the tongue or gums, or bad breath
• eyes for discharge, cloudiness, or discolored "whites"

*A healthy dog is an able companion.*

• ears for foul odor, redness, discharge, or crusted tips
• nose for thickened or colored discharge
• skin for parasites, hair loss, crusts, red spots, or lumps
• feet for cuts, abrasions, split nails, bumps, or misaligned toes
• anal region for redness, swelling, discharge, or tracts
In addition:
• Watch your dog for signs of lameness or incoordination, sore neck, circling, loss of muscling, and for any behavioral change.
• Run your hands over the muscles and bones and check that they are symmetrical from one side to the other.
• Weigh your dog and observe whether he is gaining or losing.
• Check for any growths, swellings, sores, or pigmented lumps.
• Look out for mammary masses, changes in testicle size, discharge from the vulva or penis, increased or decreased urination, foul-smelling or strangely colored urine, incontinence, swollen abdomen, black or bloody stool, change in appetite or water consumption, difficulty

*A healthy Golden is full of energy and ideas.*

breathing, lethargy, coughing, gagging, or loss of balance.

## Signs of a Healthy Golden

Understanding the normal values for your dog will help you detect when something isn't right.

**Gum color:** The simplest yet most overlooked checkpoint is your dog's gum color. Looking at the gums is so simple, yet virtually no one does it, except your veterinarian, who will look at the gums before anything else when your dog comes into the examination room sick. Be aware of the following points.

• Normal gum color is a good deep pink.

• Pale gum color can indicate anemia or poor circulation.

• White or very light gum color can indicate shock, severe anemia, or very poor circulation.

• Bluish gum or tongue color indicates imminent life-threatening lack of oxygen.

• Bright red gum color can indicate carbon monoxide poisoning.

• Yellowish color can indicate jaundice.

• Little tiny red splotches (called petechiae) can indicate a blood-clotting problem.

Don't confuse a red line around the gum line with healthy gums. A dog with dirty teeth can have gum disease, giving an unhealthy, but rosy, glow to the gums, especially at the margins around the teeth.

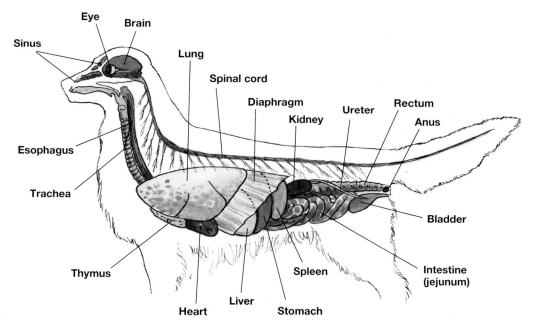

Eye
Brain
Sinus
Lung
Spinal cord
Diaphragm
Ureter
Rectum
Kidney
Anus
Esophagus
Trachea
Bladder
Thymus
Spleen
Intestine (jejunum)
Heart
Liver
Stomach

*Internal organs.*

Besides color, capillary refill time, which is an index of blood circulation, can be estimated simply by pressing on the gum with your finger and lifting your finger off. The gum where you pressed will be momentarily white, but will quickly re-pink as the blood moves back into the area. If it takes longer than a couple of seconds to re-pink, circulation is poor.

**Body temperature:** Your dog's body temperature is another clue to what's going on internally. As in humans, temperature will be slightly lower in the morning and higher in the evening. Normal temperature for a Golden is about 100 to 102°F (37.8 to 38.9°C). If the temperature is:

- 103°F (39°C) or above, call the veterinarian for advice.
- 105°F (40.6°C) or above, go to the emergency veterinarian. A temperature of 106°F (41°C) and above is dangerous.

---

**G O L D   N U G G E T**

### Check for Dehydration

To check your dog's hydration, pick up the skin on the back just above the shoulders, so that it makes a slight tent above the body. It should "pop" back into place almost immediately. If it remains tented and separated from the body, your dog is dehydrated.

---

# GOLD NUGGET

## Blood Tests

*CBC reports:*

• Red blood cells: The cells responsible for carrying oxygen throughout the body.

• White blood cells: The infection fighting cells.

• Platelets: Components responsible for clotting blood to stop bleeding.

*Blood Chemistry Test reports:*

• Albumin (ALB): Reduced levels are suggestive of liver or kidney disease, or parasites.

• Alanine aminotransferase (ALT): Elevated levels suggest liver disease.

• Alkaline phosphatase (ALKP): Elevated levels can indicate liver disease or Cushing's syndrome.

• Amylase (AMYL): Elevated levels suggest pancreatic or kidney disease.

• Blood urea nitrogen (BUN): Elevated levels suggest kidney disease or dehydration.

• Calcium (CA): Elevated levels suggest kidney or parathyroid disease or some types of tumors.

• Cholesterol (CHOL): Elevated levels suggest liver or kidney disease or several other disorders.

• Creatinine (CREA): Elevated levels suggest kidney disease or urinary obstruction.

• Blood Glucose (GLU): Low levels can suggest liver disease.

• Phosphorus (PHOS): Elevated levels can suggest kidney disease.

• Total bilirubin (TBIL): Level can indicate problems in the bile ducts.

• Total protein (TP): Level can indicate problems of the liver, kidney, or gastrointestinal tract.

---

• 98°F (36.7°C) or below, call the veterinarian.

• 96°F (35.6°C) or below, go to the emergency veterinarian.

**Pulse:** The easiest way to check your dog's pulse is to feel the pulse through the femoral artery. If your dog is standing, cup your hand around the top of the leg and feel around the inside of it, almost where it joins with the torso. If your dog is on his back, you can sometimes even see the pulse in this area. Normal pulse rate for a Golden at rest is about 60 to 120 beats per minute.

You can feel your dog's heart beat by placing your hand on his lower rib cage just behind the elbow. Don't be alarmed if it seems irregular; the heartbeat of many dogs is irregular compared to humans. Have your veterinarian check it out, then get used to how it feels when it is normal.

**Blood tests:** Your Golden's blood can provide valuable clues about his state of health. Blood tests are vital before your pet undergoes surgery to ensure that he is healthy enough for the procedure. The most common tests are the Complete Blood

Count (CBC) and the Blood Chemistry Test (Chem panel). Many other specialized tests are fairly common.

For a discussion of deworming and vaccinations, see Chapter Twelve.

## First Aid in the Field

Never let your dog loose in any area you haven't first checked out thoroughly, and never go into the field unprepared. Always have a first aid kit available, along with a means of transportation to and communication with an emergency clinic. Follow the directions outlined under the specific emergencies, call ahead to the clinic, and then transport the dog to get professional attention.

**Drowning:** If possible, hold the dog upside down by grasping him around the waist and letting his head hang toward the ground. Let the dog

*G O L D   N U G G E T*

**The First Aid Kit**
• rectal thermometer
• scissors
• tweezers
• sterile gauze dressings
• self-adhesive bandage (such as Vet-Wrap)
• instant cold compress
• antidiarrhea medication
• ophthalmic ointment
• soap
• antiseptic skin ointment
• hydrogen peroxide
• clean sponge
• penlight
• syringe
• towel
• first aid instructions
• veterinarian and emergency clinic numbers

*Always be prepared for excitement, adventure—and danger—when in the field.*

# GOLD NUGGET

## Artificial Respiration

1. Open the mouth, clear the passage of secretions and foreign bodies, and pull the tongue forward.
2. Seal your mouth over the dog's nose and mouth. Blow into the dog's nose for two seconds, then release.
3. If you don't see the chest expand, blow harder, then make a tighter seal around the lips, or check for an obstruction.
4. Repeat at a rate of one breath every four seconds, stopping every minute to monitor breathing and pulse.
5. If air collects in the stomach, push down just behind the rib cage every few minutes.

sway back and forth so that water can run out of his mouth, then administer artificial respiration, with the dog's head positioned lower than his lungs.

**Heatstroke:** Early signs of heatstroke include rapid, loud breathing, abundant thick saliva, bright red mucous membranes, and high rectal temperature. Later signs include unsteadiness, diarrhea, and coma.

Wet the dog down and place him in front of a fan. If this is not possible, immerse the dog in cool water. *Do not plunge the dog in ice water;* the resulting constriction of peripheral blood vessels can make the situation worse. Offer small amounts of water for drinking.

You must lower your dog's body temperature quickly, but you don't want the temperature to go below 100°F (37.8°C). Stop cooling the dog when the rectal temperature reaches 103°F (39°C) because it will continue to fall.

Even after the dog seems fully recovered, do not allow him to exert himself for at least three days following the incident. Hyperthermia can cause lasting effects that can result in death unless the dog is fully recovered.

*Pressure points on a Golden Retriever.*

**Hypothermia:** An excessively chilled dog will shiver and act sluggish. With continued chilling the body temperature may fall below 95°F (35°C), the pulse and breathing rates slow, and the dog may become comatose.

Warm the dog gradually by wrapping him in a blanket that has been warmed in the dryer. Place plastic milk or soda bottles filled with hot water outside the blankets, not touching the dog. You can also place a plastic tarp over the blanket, making sure the dog's head is not covered. Monitor the temperature. Stop warming when the temperature reaches 101°F (38.3°C). Monitor for shock even after the temperature has returned to normal.

**Bleeding:** Consider wounds to be an emergency if there is profuse bleeding, if they are extremely deep or large, or if they open to the chest cavity, abdominal cavity, or head.

• If possible, elevate the wound site, and apply a cold pack to it.

• Do not remove impaled objects; seek veterinary attention.

• Cover the wound with clean dressing and apply pressure. Don't remove blood-soaked bandages; apply more dressings over them until bleeding stops.

• If the wound is on an extremity, apply pressure to the closest pressure point. For a front leg, press the inside of the leg just above the elbow; for a rear leg, press the inside of the thigh where the femoral artery crosses the thighbone; for the tail, press the underside of the tail close to where it joins the body.

---

*G O L D   N U G G E T*

## CPR

1. Place your hands, one on top of the other, on the left side of the chest about 2 inches (5 cm) up from and behind the point of the elbow.
2. Press down quickly and release.
3. Compress at a rate of about 100 times per minute.
4. After every 15 compressions, give two breaths through the nose. If you have a partner, the partner can give breaths every two or three compressions.

---

• Use a tourniquet only in life-threatening situations and only when all other attempts have failed. Check for signs of shock.

• For abdominal wounds, place a warm, wet, sterile dressing over any protruding internal organs, and cover with a bandage or towel. Do not attempt to push organs back into the dog.

• For head wounds, apply gentle pressure to control bleeding. Monitor for loss of consciousness or shock and treat accordingly.

• For animal bites, allow some bleeding, then clean the area thoroughly and apply antibiotic ointment. A course of oral antibiotics will probably be necessary. It's best not to suture most animal bites, but a large one, over ½ inch (12.7 mm) in diameter, or one on the face or other prominent position, may need to be sutured.

**Limb fractures:** Lameness associated with extreme pain, swelling or deformation of the affected leg, or grinding or popping sounds, could indicate a break or another serious problem. Attempts to immobilize fractures with splints tend to do more harm than good, so it's best to keep the dog still and cushion the limb from further trauma without splinting if you can get to the veterinarian right away.

**Snakebite:** Poisonous snakebites are characterized by swelling, discoloration, pain, fangmarks, restlessness, nausea, and weakness. Most bites are to the head, and are difficult to treat with first aid. The best first aid is to keep the dog quiet and take him to the veterinarian immediately. Antivenin is the treatment of choice.

**Insect stings and allergic reactions:** Insects often sting dogs on the face or feet. Remove any visible stingers as quickly as possible by brushing them with a credit card or stiff paper; grasping a stinger often injects more venom into the dog. Administer a paste of baking soda and water to bee stings, and vinegar to wasp stings. Clean the area and apply antibacterial ointment.

Call your veterinarian immediately if you think the dog may be having a severe reaction. Insect stings are the most common cause of extreme allergic reactions in dogs. Swelling around the nose and throat can block the airway. Other possible reactions include restlessness, vomiting, diarrhea, seizures, and collapse. If any of these symptoms occur, immediate veterinary attention will probably be necessary.

# Nonemergency Injuries

More often, the injuries sustained in the field will be minor. Some, however, can ultimately be quite serious if they aren't treated.

**Foxtails:** Foxtails are barbed seeds that can cause serious problems to dogs. Once embedded in or inhaled by a dog, the seed's barbs allow it to migrate through the dog's body, sometimes causing abscesses and sometimes even entering vital organs. Symptoms include localized infections or apparent pain, irritation to the nose, eyes, or ears, and strange behaviors involving rubbing and licking parts of the dog's own body. The most common site of migration is the external ear canal, involving about half of all cases. Other common sites include the webbing between the toes, eye, nose, lumbar area, and thoracic cavity. Foxtails usually have to be removed under anesthesia.

**Foot injuries:** Burrs, cuts, peeled pads, broken nails, or other foot injuries can cause lameness. Cuts and peeled pads should be carefully flushed with warm water, and an antibacterial ointment applied. Cover the area with gauze, then wrap the foot with Vet-Wrap, a stretchable bandage that clings to itself. You can also add padding. Change the dressing twice daily, or anytime it gets wet, and restrict exercise until it heals.

If you need a quick fix for a minor injury, you can fashion a makeshift pad by attaching a thin piece of rubber or leather to the bottom of the pad with Super-Glue, or you can apply a coat of Nu-Skin, available at drug stores, if the injury is not too extensive. Peeled pads are very painful. A local anesthetic such as hemorrhoid cream or a topical toothache salve can help ease some of the discomfort. Deep cuts or extensive peeling should be checked by your veterinarian for foreign objects or tendon damage.

A split nail can be treated by cutting it as short as possible and soaking it in warm saltwater. Apply an antibiotic and then a human fingernail mender, followed by a bandage.

If a toe is swollen, does not match its fellow on the opposite foot in shape and position, makes a grinding sound when moved, or if the dog is in considerable pain, he should be kept quiet and checked by your veterinarian. Meanwhile minimize swelling by applying cold packs or placing the foot in a bucket of cold water.

**Tail problems:** Several hunting breeds, including Golden Retrievers, are prone to a peculiar tail problem known as "dead," "cold," or "limber" tail, in which a dog will suddenly have a tail that seems paralyzed. The dog can't lift or wag its tail, and the base of the tail seems to be quite painful. The tail may extend horizontally for a few inches and then drop straight down. Owners often assume the dog has broken its tail, but radiographs reveal no broken bones. Most dogs that have this problem were either given a bath, went swimming, spent the previous day hunting while wagging or using their tail a lot, or were transported in a cage within the past day. The cause is unknown; some evidence suggests that excessive use of the tail causes inflammation and swelling of the surrounding tissues, which, in turn, press upon the nerves

## GOLD NUGGET

### Dewclaws

Many breeders elect to remove the dewclaws, the thumblike toes on the dog's front wrists, a few days after birth. Some dogs, especially field dogs, have experienced painful and recurring injuries when their dewclaws were ripped off after being caught on brambles, and must ultimately have them removed under anesthesia as adults. Not all dogs have this problem, and it may have to do with how tightly the dewclaw grows on the leg. Some breeders object to the practice of removal because they feel it weakens the pastern, and can be especially detrimental in jumping dogs. Dogs with dewclaws should have them checked regularly, and extra care should be taken to keep the nail short. They can be wrapped with veterinary cling wrap (such as "Vet-Wrap") as a precaution in the field.

*Your dog doesn't have to be a field trial competitor to push himself to the limit.*

The condition usually lasts a few days but may last a couple of weeks; some dogs seem to get it time after time, whereas others have only a single episode in their life.

## Joint Problems

Joints occur at the moving junction of two bones. The ends of the bones are covered with cartilage, which helps to cushion impact and allows for smoother movement between the bones. The joint is enclosed by the joint capsule, the inner layer of which is the synovial membrane. The synovial membrane produces synovial fluid, a thick liquid that fills the joint cavity and provides lubrication and nourishment. Cartilage can be injured from excessive joint stress or from any preexisting joint instability, allowing the bones to bump together abnormally. Injured cartilage releases enzymes that break down the normally thick synovial fluid into a thin fluid that neither lubricates nor nourishes adequately, in turn resulting in further cartilage deterioration. If the dog continues to stress the joint, damage will increase until it extends to the joint capsule and bone. Only at this point are sensory nerves affected so that the dog feels pain. This means that considerable joint damage has already been done by the time your dog exhibits lameness from a preexisting condition.

**Synovitis:** Active dogs can subject their joints to excessive forces, stretching the joint capsule and

leading to the tail. Some preliminary research suggests affected dogs have elevated muscle enzymes, consistent with the sore muscles that people get after a hard workout. This does not explain the relationship to bathing, however, which seems to occur with both warm and cold water. One suggestion to prevent dead tail is to dry the tail thoroughly (even using a blow dryer) after the dog works in water or is bathed, and to avoid placing the dog in cramped quarters after it has been working. No treatment exists, although some owners feel that giving an antiinflammatory drug may help.

*G O L D   N U G G E T*

**Hereditary Joint Problems**
See pages 79 and 82 for an overview of hip and elbow dysplasia, osteochondritis dessecans, and panosteitis.

inflaming the surrounding soft tissue. Small blood vessels in the tissue dilate and the vessel walls leak fluid into the joint cavity. This influx of excess fluid causes swelling and pain, a condition recognized as synovitis. Continued synovitis leads to an inflammatory response that damages the articular cartilage and its ability to act as a shock absorber. Eventually, the loss of cushioning can lead to irreparable damage to the bony component of the joint.

**Arthritis:** In older dogs, or dogs with a previous injury, limping is often the result of degenerative joint disease (DJD), more commonly called arthritis. In some dogs, there is no obvious cause. In others, abnormal stresses or trauma to the joint can cause degeneration of the joint cartilage and underlying bone. The synovial membrane surrounding the joint becomes inflamed and the bone develops small bony outgrowths called osteophytes. These changes cause the joint to stiffen, become painful, and have decreased range of motion. In cases in which an existing condition is exacerbating the DJD, surgery to remedy the condition is warranted.

When considering surgery for a joint problem, keep in mind that the more the joint is used in its damaged state, the more DJD will occur. Even though the surgery may fix the initial problem, if too much damage has occurred, the dog will still be plagued with incurable arthritic changes. Prevention of arthritis is the key.

Conservative treatment entails keeping the dog's weight down,

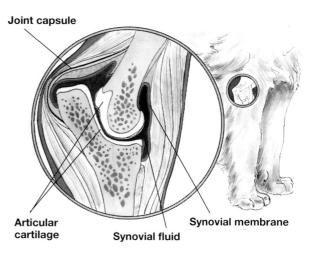

Joint capsule

Articular cartilage

Synovial fluid

Synovial membrane

*A normal joint.*

attending to injuries, and maintaining a program of exercise. Low-impact exercise such as walking or swimming every other day is best for dogs with signs of arthritis. Newer drugs, such as carprofen, are available from your veterinarian and may help alleviate some of the symptoms of DJD, but they should be used only with careful veterinary supervision. Some newer drugs and supplements may actually improve the joint. Polysulfated glycosaminoglycan increases the compressive resilience of cartilage. Glucosamine stimulates the synthesis of collagen, and may help rejuvenate cartilage to some extent. Chondroitin sulfate helps to shield cartilage from destructive enzymes.

**Ruptured cruciate ligament:** Ligaments provide stability to joints by connecting one bone to another. They are made of dense connective tissue that becomes less elastic with

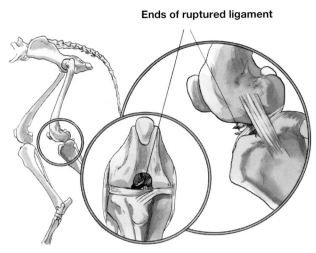

**Ends of ruptured ligament**

*Ruptured cruciate ligament.*

age; when stretched by more than about 10 percent, tearing occurs. The anterior cruciate ligament prevents the stifle joint from slipping from side to side, and injuries to it are common in large or overweight dogs. Injuries occur most often during jumping or acceleration, from a strong sideways force, or for no clear reason. Because most cruciate tears don't get well on their own, they usually require surgery, even if they are only partial tears. The instability in the stifle caused by the torn cruciate ligament causes further damage to the surrounding medial meniscus, which may or may not have also torn with the initial injury. This torn meniscus will often produce a clicking noise when the dog is walking or trotting. Without stabilization, degenerative changes will cause the joint to become arthritic.

Several methods of surgical repair are in use; intracapsular repair is usu-

ally the choice for Golden Retrievers. In this surgery, the joint is first cleaned out, removing any remnants of the meniscus and damaged ligament. This prevents further degenerative changes and allows the meniscus to regenerate. The ligament is replaced by a graft or synthetic material, over which the body produces collagen to form a regenerated ligament. None of these regenerated structures is as strong as the original, but they are better than the damaged one. If a dog has torn cruciate ligaments of both legs, one leg is usually given a temporary extracapsular repair, in which the joint is stabilized by suturing around the joint capsule. This technique may be appropriate as a permanent surgery for very old and inactive dogs, as it is easier and recovery is faster. Intracapsular cruciate surgery requires a commitment to careful nursing; postoperatively, the dog must be kept still for one to two months, and then gradually allowed controlled exercise. Even newer cruciate repair techniques may hold promise; consult a veterinarian familiar with orthopedic surgeries.

# Lameness Therapies

A veterinarian should examine any lameness that persists without significant improvement after three days of complete rest. Ice packs may help minimize swelling if applied immediately after an injury, but remember that

*With proper care most Goldens can return to active lives after injuries.*

prolonged direct contact—more than 15 minutes—can damage the skin. In fact, anytime you use an ice pack you should place a thin cloth between it and the skin. The reduced tissue temperature lowers the metabolic rate and inhibits edema and the sensation of pain. Cold therapy can be helpful for up to a week following an injury.

Heat therapy can be beneficial to older injuries. Heat increases the metabolic rate of the tissue, relaxes muscle spasms, and can provide some pain relief. Moist heat applied for about 20-minute periods is preferable, and care must be taken to avoid burning. Other types of heat therapy are available that penetrate more deeply through the tissues, but because they also carry a greater risk of burn injury, they should be performed only by an experienced person.

Complete rest and total inactivity are the best initial home care for any lameness. Rest your dog well past the time he stops limping. Exercise therapy is equally important, but exercise must be controlled. Leash walking and swimming are excellent low-impact exercises for recovering dogs.

In many injuries in which the limb must be rested, passive motion can be important in preventing muscle contraction and maintaining the health of the joint. All movements should be slow and well within the joint's normal range of motion. Massage therapy can be useful for loosening tendons and increasing circulation.

Many injuries are quite painful and may require drug therapy for pain relief. Orthopedic surgeries can be particularly painful and almost always warrant analgesics. Pain has a self-perpetuating aspect, which means that it is easier to prevent than to stop. Discuss with your veterinarian the pros and cons of various analgesics.

# Chapter Seven
# Heredity and Health

It is a fact of life that every dog of any breed carries some recessive deleterious genes in its makeup. Golden Retrievers, like all breeds, have a limited gene pool that descends from a fairly small number of ancestral foundation dogs. In fact, it has been estimated that 99 percent of current Goldens trace back to three breeding pairs: Ch Heydown Gunner bred to Onaway in 1924, Binks of Kentford bred to Balvaig in 1921, and Rory of Bentley bred to Aurora in 1924 and 1925. Even behind these dogs there was a limited pool of founding Goldens. It was inevitable that a founding dog would carry a deleterious gene; if that gene was for a serious health problem, especially one not evident until later life, after dogs have already reproduced, that problem can eventually become widespread in the breed. Careless breeding increases the incidence of these problems, but even carefully bred dogs can be affected. In Goldens, their hereditary burden includes a

*New diagnostics, and new treatments, are on the horizon. Don't turn your back on hereditary health problems.*

couple of major problems and several minor ones.

## Skeletal Disorders

Hereditary joint problems are prevalent in many breeds, with elbow and hip dysplasia being the most widespread. Golden Retrievers have both. The mode of inheritance is unknown, but seem to be consistent with polygenic traits—traits that depend upon the interaction of several different genes. This means a dog is more likely to be unaffected if its ancestors were unaffected, but even then there are no guarantees.

### Hip Dysplasia
Hip dysplasia (HD) occurs when the ball of the femur (thigh) bone does not fit properly in the socket (acetabulum) of the pelvic bone. The fit is affected by both the depth and shape of the socket and the laxity of the joint. With pressure on the joint, such as that occurring when the dog walks or runs, the combination of a shallow socket and joint laxity allows the ball of the femur to pop in and out of the socket. This movement

further deteriorates the socket's rim, worsening the condition and advancing degenerative joint disease. This is why early diagnosis and treatment are important.

Hip radiographs can detect HD before outward signs are noticeable. In the United States, radiographs are usually rated by either the Orthopedic Foundation for Animals (OFA) or the Pennsylvania Hip Improvement Program (PennHIP). Breeders disagree about which method is better; therefore, many breeders elect to have two radiographs taken at the same time, submitting one to each registry. The only bad choice is no certification at all.

**OFA:** The OFA is the older and more popular hip registry. The dog must be positioned on her back with her legs parallel to each other and the surface, and then rotated so the patellas (kneecaps) are situated on top of the stifle. This requires either a sedated or very cooperative dog. A panel of specialists subjectively rates radiographs according to several specific joint characteristics. A dog with "normal" hips, which includes ratings of excellent, good, and fair, receives an OFA number. Borderline ratings indicate that a dog should be rechecked in another six to eight months. Dysplastic hips include ratings of mild, moderate,

*The best way to produce healthy pups is to breed from healthy parents who have tested free of hereditary health problems.*

and severe. Approximately 22 percent of Golden Retriever radiographs submitted to the OFA are judged dysplastic. Ratings are not given until dogs are two years old, but preliminary ratings can be obtained before then. It's a good idea to have your Golden's hips evaluated at an early age so that you can take measures to prevent irreparable joint changes, which may include surgery or simply administration of glucosamine and chondroitin sulfate.

**PennHIp:** PennHIp evaluation must be performed on an anesthetized dog, and consists of three views of the hips. The first is like the standard OFA view; the others are taken with the legs positioned perpendicular to the dog, as though in a standing position. The first of these is taken with the femur pushed in to deeply seat it in the acetabulum, and the second is taken with the femur pushed outward so that it is loosely seated in the acetabulum. The difference between the two views is measured as a Distraction Index (DI) ranging from 0.0 to 1.0, with lower numbers reflecting tighter (better) hips. At this time, insufficient data exist to determine at what point the DI in a Golden is considered dysplastic, but preliminary evidence in other breeds suggests that dogs with a DI greater than 0.3 will develop signs of dysplasia and degenerative joint disease. There is evidence that abnormal hips can be detected at a younger age with the PennHIp method.

**GOLD NUGGET**

**OFA Numbers**
A dog with normal hips receives an OFA number, such as GR1333G24MT, in which GR stands for Golden Retriever, 1333 means this dog is the 1333rd Golden to receive an OFA number, the G stands for "good" (it could also be F for fair or E for excellent), the 24 stands for the dog's age in months when x-rayed, the M stands for male (F for female), and the T stands for tattooed (M stands for microchipped).

**Treatment:** Hip dysplasia can become progressively more crippling and painful. Whereas mild cases may not need specific treatment, more severe cases may need timely

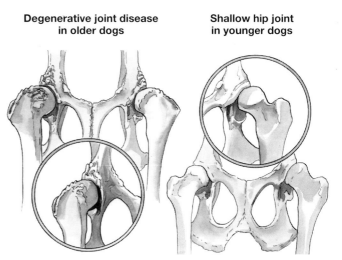

**Degenerative joint disease in older dogs**

**Shallow hip joint in younger dogs**

*Hip dysplasia.*

*Healthy joints enable Goldens to spend active lives.*

surgery in order to prevent crippling disability. If the condition is detected in a young dog before secondary changes (osteoarthrosis) have occurred, a procedure called a triple pelvic osteotomy (TPO) can be performed. In a TPO, the orientation of the dog's hip socket is surgically changed, allowing the femur head to fit better into the socket. Older dogs or dogs with more advanced dysplasia are better candidates for a total hip replacement, in which the ball of the femur is replaced with a metallic ball, and the socket is replaced with a Teflon cup. A third procedure, which is less effective in large dogs,

is to simply remove the head of the femur. It might be a reasonable choice for financial reasons in an older dog that needs only to be comfortable walking around the house.

## Elbow Dysplasia

Elbow dysplasia encompasses several problems, all of which eventually lead to degenerative joint disease of the elbow. The most common causes are fragmented coronoid process (FCP), ununited anconeal process, and osteochondrosis dessecans (OCD) of the condyle of the humerus. In Golden Retrievers, fragmented coronoid process is the most common cause seen in reports submitted to the OFA.

FCP often occurs together with OCD of the same joint. The medial coronoid process of the ulna is a thin finger of bone that normally attaches to the head of the ulna, one of the long bones of the forearm. It works to stabilize the elbow by fitting snugly in a notch in the humerus (upper arm) where it hinges with the ulna. In some dogs, the coronoid process never attaches properly to the ulna or becomes fragmented, allowing the dog's elbow to shift from side to side when the dog places weight upon it. The fragments break loose, float around, and irritate the elbow.

Symptoms, which can appear in dogs as young as seven months of age, include varying degrees of swelling, pain, and lameness originating in the elbow joint. Affected dogs have a decreased range of elbow motion, which can be tested by holding the dog's wrist and pressing the top of the wrist toward the point of shoulder, the joint between the scapula and humerus. The distance between the point of shoulder and the dog's forearm should be within about 1 inch (2.5 cm) of touching. A greater distance indicates a decreased range of motion and suggests an elbow problem. Radiographs (X rays) can more accurately diagnose the condition; however, FCP can be easy to miss unless the dog is positioned just right for the fragments to show up. Treatment is by surgical removal of the loose frag-

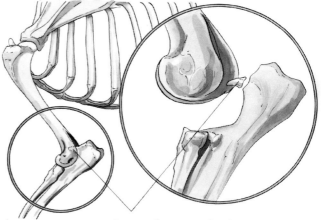

Anconeal process that has failed to unite with the ulna.

*Elbow dysplasia.*

ments, although secondary arthritis can still cause lameness.

**OFA registry:** The OFA maintains a registry for elbows, and all Golden breeding stock should have an OFA elbow clearance. Dogs over two years of age with normal elbows are assigned a breed registry number. Abnormal elbows are assigned either Grade I, II, or III, with Grade III being the most severely affected. Just over 10 percent of Golden elbow radiographs submitted to OFA are rated dysplastic.

## Osteochondrosis Dissecans

Osteochondrosis dissecans (OCD) is lameness that occurs when a flap of cartilage becomes detached from the bone. Lameness is progressive and often starts around seven to ten months of age. The most common site is in one or both shoulders, but almost any joint

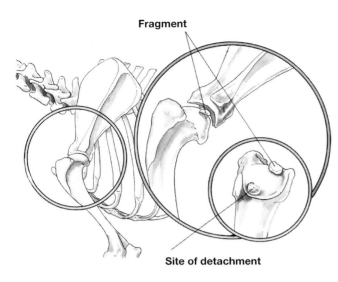

Fragment

Site of detachment

*OCD of the shoulder.*

can be affected. Often, absolute rest for several weeks can help, although sometimes lameness may seem to actually worsen with rest. Symptoms seem better with mild exercise, and worse with heavy exercise. Surgical repair is usually preferable, and is especially satisfying with OCD of the shoulder.

### Panosteitis

Panosteitis is an inflammation of the long bones resulting in lameness, which often shifts from leg to leg. "Pano" is most common in growing dogs of large breeds, including Goldens. Symptoms may appear suddenly, usually between five and ten months of age. The exact cause is not known, but the prognosis for a full recovery is excellent. Meanwhile, treatment consists of limiting exercise and administering analgesics.

# Ocular Disorders

Breeding stock should be checked by a veterinary ophthalmologist and cleared by the Canine Eye Registration Foundation (CERF). Certification is good for only a year because of the progressive nature of most eye diseases, necessitating yearly exams for convincing evidence of ocular health.

### Juvenile Cataracts

The lens lies behind the pupil and iris of the eye and focuses the light on the retina. Many dogs get cataracts (opacities of the lens) as they age, but in some Goldens, cataracts can appear at a young age, usually before they are seven years old. These cataracts, called juvenile cataracts, are usually hereditary. Typical juvenile cataracts of the Golden Retriever are on the back of the lens and grow in a roughly triangular shape, along the lens' natural suture lines. Suture lines are Y-shaped lines on the lens that are a natural result of the way the lens grows. Some Goldens have prominent Y-sutures that can be mistaken for early stage cataracts. Unlike cataracts, however, prominent Y-sutures do not grow in severity and do not interfere with vision. Even juvenile cataracts aren't usually extensive and don't interfere with the dog's vision, although they do tend to get progressively worse with age. In severe cases, the lens can be removed and replaced with a prosthetic lens.

## Retinal Dysplasia

Retinal dysplasia (RD) is a defect of the retina in which two of the retinal layers fail to grow together properly during development. As a congenital condition, it gets neither better nor worse with age, and can be detected in even young (cooperative) puppies. Sometimes, RD is mild, so that the usually smooth retinal layer has "retinal folds." In more severe cases the affected area will be much larger, resulting in "geographic" RD. At its worst, the two layers remain separated throughout the eye and retinal detachment occurs. The mode of inheritance is not known, and in some cases, prenatal infections can play a role.

## Central PRA

Central Progressive Retinal Atrophy (CPRA) is similar to, but separate from, Progressive Retinal Atrophy (PRA). In CPRA the light-sensitive cells of the center part of the retina gradually deteriorate. As more of these cells are lost, the dog's vision gets gradually worse, ultimately resulting in blindness. Researchers have recently identified vitamin E as playing an important role in this disorder. Vitamin E is an anitoxidant that helps protect the retinal cells from damage caused by light. Affected dogs don't seem to retain vitamin E in their system in sufficient quantities after they ingest it. Experimental studies suggest that by supplementing these dogs with vitamin E, sufficient levels of vitamin E can be maintained in the dog's system to

*G O L D    N U G G E T*

**CERF numbers**

A CERF number looks something like this: CERF GR3456/99-36. The GR stands for Golden Retriever, the 3456 indicates it was the 3,456th Golden registered with CERF, 99 is the year of the latest clear examination, and the 36 is the age in months of the dog at that time.

protect the retina and prevent CPRA. Prevention will still involve careful screening, since the problem must be caught early in order to stop the disease progression.

## Lid and Lash Disorders

The most common eye disorders in all dogs are probably those of the

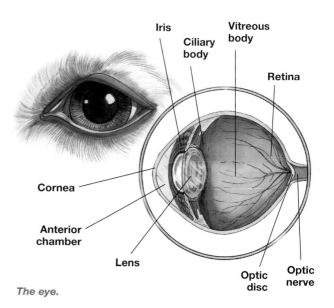

*The eye.*

*Good ocular health is important for your dog's comfort and happiness.*

lids and lashes. Dogs with deep-set or diamond-shaped eyes are more likely to have entropion, in which the eyelids turn in toward the eye. This allows the lashes to rub against, irritate, and even damage the eye. In ectropion, the lid is turned outward, leading to drying and irritation of the eye and surrounding tissues. In trichiasis and distichiasis, the eyelashes are directed in toward the eye, irritating it. In many of these disorders, surgery may be needed for the dog's health and comfort.

## Circulatory System Disorders

Compared to many other breeds, Goldens have healthy circulatory systems, but they, too, have their baggage. All breeding stock should be examined by a veterinary cardiologist, and even nonbreeding dogs should be screened by having a veterinarian listen to (auscultate) the heart for a murmur. Heart murmurs indicate a turbulent blood flow, usually the result of blood being forced

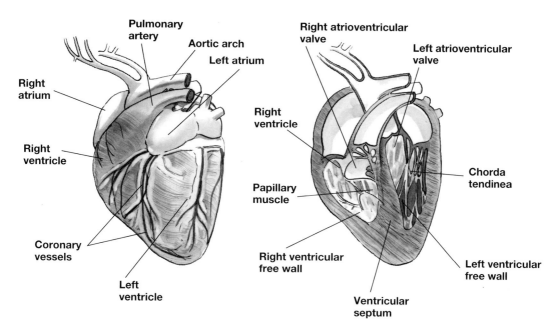

**Right atrium**

**Pulmonary artery**

**Aortic arch**

**Left atrium**

**Right ventricle**

**Coronary vessels**

**Left ventricle**

**Right atrioventricular valve**

**Left atrioventricular valve**

**Right ventricle**

**Papillary muscle**

**Right ventricular free wall**

**Ventricular septum**

**Chorda tendinea**

**Left ventricular free wall**

*A normal heart.*

through a faulty heart valve or through too small an opening. They are graded from I to VI in severity, with VI being worst. Dogs with murmurs, especially those above grade II, should be seen by a veterinary cardiologist for an ultrasound of the heart.

## Subvalvular Aortic Stenosis

Subvalvular aortic stenosis (SAS) is one of the most common congenital heart defects in dogs, and one of the breeds that it is seen most often in is the Golden Retriever. In SAS, the opening between the heart's left ventricle and aorta is abnormally narrow, obstructing the blood flow. Severe cases cause death by three years of age. Less severe cases may not exhibit noticeable signs, although

some dogs may be weak and collapse when exercising. Screening diagnosis is done by auscultation.

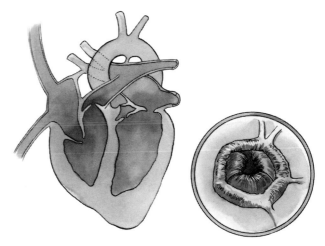

*A heart with aortic stenosis (inset).*

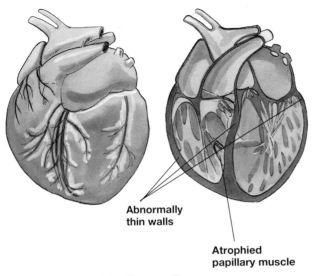

Abnormally
thin walls

Atrophied
papillary muscle

*A heart with dilated cardiomyopathy.*

Detection of a resting heart murmur—one present when the dog is at rest—calls for further diagnostic tests by a veterinary cardiologist. Doppler ultrasound can measure the extra turbulence and velocity of the blood caused by it being forced through the narrow opening; a velocity of at least 2.0 meters per second has been used as an approximate threshold for suspecting a dog has SAS. If a Golden has both a resting heart murmur and a high Doppler velocity, it is considered to have SAS. Some dogs fall into a questionable category. These dogs may have a softer (grade I or II) murmur, or a murmur detectable only after exercise, and the blood velocity may be raised but not quite to the established threshold.

Some Golden breeders have found discrepancies in diagnoses between cardiologists. For this rea-

son, it may be prudent to get a second or even third opinion before removing a valuable dog from a breeding program. This is not, however, an excuse to "shop around" for a more favorable diagnosis in order to obtain a health clearance on a questionable dog.

An affected dog should not be bred. Current evidence is consistent with the idea that SAS is hereditary, and that it is inherited as a dominant trait with variable expressivity. This means that some dogs with the gene may have little, if any, symptoms of SAS but can still pass it on. Such dogs are known as "silent" or "occult" cases. SAS can lead to early, or even sudden, death and is not a disease to risk. For serious cases, open-heart surgery is the best treatment, but it is expensive and risky.

## Dilated Cardiomyopathy

Dilated Cardiomyopathy (DCM) is a progressive disease in which the muscles of the heart lose their contractility. The heart compensates by several mechanisms that ultimately produce an enlarged heart with thin muscle walls. Symptoms include coughing, labored or rapid breathing, weight loss, general debilitation, abdominal distention, cold extremities, fainting episodes, and heart murmur. Often, symptoms appear to have developed quite suddenly. This is especially true in dogs that are normally not very active, but, in fact, the condition has been developing slowly; only when the failing heart can no longer compensate, do the symptoms surface. Definitive diagnosis is with an electrocardiogram and ultrasound.

Cardiomyopathy is one of the most common serious acquired cardiac diseases in dogs. When considered as a percentage, Goldens rank fourteenth out of all breeds. In most breeds, there is no prevention and no cure for cardiomyopathy, and dogs eventually die of congestive heart failure or severe arrythmias (abnormal beating).

Goldens may be a little more fortunate in this respect. Some, but not all, Goldens with DCM have abnormally low amounts of taurine in their blood plasma. Taurine is an essential amino acid found in meat. It is important in many bodily processes, including normal heart function. In these dogs, supplementation with taurine (about 1000 mg twice a day) may significantly improve the condition, and is at least worth a try.

## von Willebrand's Disease

Canine von Willebrand's Disease (vWD) is a hereditary deficiency in one of the clotting factors that can lead to excessive bleeding. Blood clotting depends not only on a sufficient number of platelets in the blood, but also on a chain of chemical reactions of molecules known as clotting factors. Each successive factor in the chain reaction is identified numerically; in vWD, factor VIII is abnormal or deficient. The degree of deficiency varies between affected individuals because of a somewhat randomized factor in the nature of the mutation that causes it. Dogs with only a slight deficiency will have few symptoms; those with a greater deficiency may have prolonged or uncontrolled bleeding during surgeries or from cuts, lameness from bleeding into the joints, hematomas (accumulations of blood beneath the skin), nosebleeds, and other abnormal bleeding.

A simple blood test is available, but the results have a great deal of fluctuation. About 10 percent of this variability is from variations in the test itself, but most of the variation is due to variations within the dog's production of von Willebrand factor. This means that a dog with a suspicious test result should be retested several times before concluding it is affected.

A DNA test is available for some breeds—but not Goldens—for vWD. In a comparison of DNA results with blood test measurements of von Willebrand factor, a significant overlap of values between DNA proven carriers and proven clear dogs was found. Again, this suggests that the blood tests are not very reliable and may need to be repeated several times for the results to be accepted with a degree of certainty.

A dog that also has hypothyroidism is more likely to have lower von Willebrand factor, so dogs with suspected vWD should be checked for thyroid function. A Golden with vWD should be treated with a drug (desmopressin acetate) that increases clotting ability prior to surgery. Although vWD has been reported in Goldens, it does not appear to be a major problem in the breed. It appears to be inherited as an incomplete dominant, so that dogs with one copy of the abnormal gene will have fewer symptoms than dogs with two copies.

# Endocrine System Disorders

The endocrine system includes several glands that secrete hormones, chemicals that travel via the bloodstream to cells and tissues in the body, regulating their function. Endocrine system disorders include diabetes, Cushing's syndrome (see page 186), Addison's disease, and others, but the main endocrine disorder diagnosed in Goldens is hypothyroidism.

## Hypothyroidism

The thyroid glands are located near the dog's Adam's apple (larynx) in the neck, and produce calcitonin, a hormone necessary for normal calcium metabolism, and thyroxine (T4), a hormone that regulates metabolism and is essential for the normal function of many of the body's organs and systems. In some dogs, the thyroid gland doesn't make enough hormones, usually because the thyroid gland degenerates from being attacked by the body's own immune system, or for other, unknown reasons.

Hypothyroidism is the most commonly seen endocrine problem in Goldens—in fact, in all purebreeds as a group—and a recent study reported it was seen more often in Goldens than in most other breeds. It is diagnosed more often in spayed and neutered dogs. However, many investigators believe hypothyroidism is overdiagnosed. This is especially true in Goldens because, as a recent study showed, clinically normal Goldens test in the lower range of normal test values. A correct diagnosis entails relating both clinical signs of the disease with laboratory test results indicative of impaired thyroid function.

Clinical signs include hair loss on the flanks, tail, or behind the ears; darkened and thickened skin, sometimes with scaling or seborrhea; weight gain, lethargy, intolerance to cold, slowed heart rate, and infertility, among others. Don't assume your Golden is hypothyroid based only on clinical signs, however.

**Tests:** The simplest test for hypothyroidism is a blood test for baseline serum T4 level. This test, however, is only recommended for identifying dogs with normal thyroid function; it should never be used as the final test to diagnose abnormal thyroid function. Dogs with T4 levels in the higher or even middle part of the normal range are probably not hypothyroid. Dogs with T4 levels in the lower part of the normal range may be in the early stages of hypothyroidism. Dogs with T4 levels below the normal range are suspected of hypothyroidism, but keep in mind that dogs that are sick, have recently undergone anesthesia, or are taking some drugs, including steroids, some nonsteroidal antiin-flammatories, and anticonvulsants, may have a misleadingly low T4 value; therefore, dogs with low T4 values should have additional testing.

More definitive tests include free T4 measured by equilibrium dialysis (fT4ed) and canine thyroid-stimulating hormone (cTSH) measurements. In the cTSH stimulation test, T4 levels are measured before and six hours after the dog is given a thyroid-stimulating hormone (TSH). A dog with a normally functioning thyroid should respond with a much higher level of T4. These tests entail greater expense, and some veterinarians suggest, in cases in which financial factors play a role, to instead begin the dog on thyroid sup-plementation, which is relatively inex-pensive, and see if the symptoms resolve. The dog is then weaned from the supplementation, and if symptoms return, the dog is diagnosed with probable hypothyroidism. The draw-back of this approach is that in the meantime, the real reason for the dog's problems may be overlooked, and some dogs are not candidates for supplementation.

**Treatment:** Treatment for hypo-thyroidism is with daily medication, and progress monitored with re-testing in about two months. It is important to perform the tests about four to six hours after thyroid med-ication is given in order to measure the peak value.

# Cancers

Cancers occur relatively fre-quently in all breeds of dogs. Some types occur with equal frequency in all breeds whereas other types occur more often only in certain breeds.

### Mast Cell Tumors

Skin cancer is the most common type of cancer in dogs, and mast cell tumors are among the most com-mon skin cancers. Golden Retrievers appear to have an increased risk of mast cell tumors compared to other breeds. Although they can appear at any age, they are most commonly diagnosed at around 8 or 9 years of age, and are also diagnosed more often in neutered and spayed dogs.

Mast cells are actually a type of blood cell involved in the body's response to inflammation and aller-gens. Mast cell tumors can appear in many parts of the body, most often the spleen, liver, bone marrow,

G O L D ★ S T A R

A medical pioneer is a Golden named Breeze, one of the first dogs trained as a Physician's Assisting Canine to sniff out skin cancers in people. Formally known as OTCh Colabaugh's Morninglo Breeze UDX, MH, NA, WCX, CGC, OD, Breeze was also the first Golden female to earn these titles.

*Most Goldens enjoy healthy lives—although there are no guarantees from even the healthiest families.*

and skin. Those of the skin are most easily discovered by owners. A mast cell tumor most often appears as a small, firm, raised mass, usually with well-defined borders. It may or may not be reddened, hairless, and ulcerated. Sometimes a mast cell tumor will continue to grow quite large, whereas others may become a diffuse area of thickened skin. Obviously, it is nearly impossible to diagnose a mast cell tumor from appearance alone.

Diagnosis begins with a biopsy, which can usually be done as a fine needle aspirate. Cancerous cells are staged from Grade 0 to Grade IV according to how well the cells are differentiated. Grade 0 carries the best prognosis. The prognosis also depends on the results of other tests, including blood tests, urinalysis, lymph node aspiration, and ultrasound of the abdomen to check for tumors of the liver and spleen. Low-grade tumors are least likely to be associated with adverse results of these other tests.

Treatment depends upon the tumor grade and other test results. A low-grade tumor can often be effectively treated by surgical excision with wide margins (removing a good deal of tissue around and beneath the tumor). Ultrasound of the tumor can better delineate the tumor margins than simply feeling for them and is suggested when possible, but even so it is not uncommon for cancerous cells to be left behind. These cells can be removed with a subsequent surgery or destroyed with radiation. Treatments typically involve radiation every other day for a month.

With higher-grade tumors, or with evidence of metastasis to other parts of the body, chemotherapy may be initiated. Prednisone is the most effective drug, and although it has several unfortunate side effects, its benefits generally far outweigh them. Because mast cells are involved in allergic reactions, antihistamines are also prescribed. Antacids are also part of the regimen because mast cells also release substances that, when released in excess, can cause gastric ulcers.

The prognosis depends upon the grade of the tumor and the presence of metastatic tumors. A low-grade tumor with no sign of metastasis carries a very good prognosis, given aggressive therapy. A high-grade tumor with signs of metastasis, unfortunately, carries a less favorable prognosis, with many dogs succumbing to symptoms of the spread cancer.

## Hemangiosarcoma

Hemangiosarcoma is a malignant cancer of the circulatory system, actually originating in the endothelium, or lining, of the blood vessels and spleen. Most often, hemangiosarcoma occurs as a tumor on the spleen or heart, or the peri-

G O L D ★ S T A R

Goldens can manage the loss of a limb amazingly well, but even so, when Torch, a Golden that lost her front leg to an animal trap, went on to earn her WC title, it lent new meaning to the word "game."

cardium (the sac surrounding the heart) although it may sometimes first appear as a skin growth. As the tumor grows, internal bleeding may occur. Affected dogs may suddenly appear disoriented and collapse, and exhibit signs of hypovolemic shock, including extreme thirst and very pale gums. Bleeding from the splenic tumors can result in a bloated, fluid-filled abdomen. Radiographs may reveal an enlarged spleen. If a tumor on the heart bleeds, the blood goes into the pericardial sac and fills it like a balloon; this condition, too, is visible with a radiograph. A better diagnostic tool in both cases is an ultrasound evaluation.

If the tumor is on the skin, it can be surgically removed and it's possible that the dog will make a full recovery as long as the cancer, which is highly malignant, has not already spread. If the tumor is on the spleen, the spleen can be removed. Not all tumors of the spleen are malignant, so it is a good idea to have a biopsy done and wait for results before making any decisions. Even small tumors near the heart can sometimes be removed,

**GOLD NUGGET**

**Also See . . .**
Goldens have an increased incidence of food allergies (see page
42), allergic skin disorders (see
page 58), hot spots (see page 59),
and ear infections (see page 60).

and the pericardial sac can be
removed or tapped to decrease the
pressure placed upon the heart by
being squeezed by the blood-filled
sac. Unfortunately, despite all surgical
and chemotherapeutic treatments,
most dogs with hemangiosarcoma
succumb within a couple of months
after diagnosis either to its primary
effects—internal bleeding that cannot
be stopped—or to cancer spread to
other organs. Many also die of dis-
seminated intravascular coagulation

(DIC), in which the blood clots inap-
propriately within the blood vessels,
which also decreases the clotting ele-
ments normally available to stop
bleeding in other locations.

In a recent comparison of heart
tumors in dogs presented to veterinary schools, Golden Retrievers
accounted for more cases of heart
tumors and hemangiosarcoma of
the heart than any other breed. Even
when the data were adjusted to
account for the fact that Goldens
made up more of the total patients,
they still ranked fifth in percentage
incidence. Spayed females had a
much higher incidence than intact
ones, but neutered and intact males
had similar incidences.

## Lymphosarcoma

One of the more commonly seen
cancers in dogs, lymphosarcoma

*Don't let hereditary health disease rob you of your best friend—-support research, and buy from tested stock.*

affects the blood and lymph systems; symptoms may include swelling of the lymph nodes, especially those of the lower neck area and behind the "knees." Chemotherapy can extend the life of many affected dogs.

### Osteosarcoma

Osteosarcoma (bone cancer) occurs more frequently in large-breed dogs, including Goldens. Owners are faced with the terrible decision of amputation that must be made quickly, as time is of the essence to prevent the spread to other parts of the body. Dogs adjust to the loss of a limb fairly easily, but factors such as age, weight, arthritis and other joint problems factor into how well the dog can cope with only three legs. The possibility of phantom limb pain can be reduced by having the veterinarian numb the leg for the day before it is to be removed. Unfortunately, even with the best of therapy, survival time for dogs with osteosarcoma may be short.

### Mammary Gland Tumors

Mammary gland tumors are among the most common of cancers in the dog, occurring mostly in females that were not spayed early in life. Spaying after the age of two years doesn't impart the protection from mammary cancer that earlier spaying does. Approximately 50 percent of all mammary tumors are malignant. Any suspicious lump in the breast should be removed for biopsy; needle aspiration can be used but is not suggested because of the possibility that malig-

nant cells could be missed in sampling. Therapy may include surgical excision and chemotherapy.

# Golden Retriever Muscular Dystrophy (GRMD)

Although a rare disorder, GRMD, as the name implies, is recognized more often in Goldens than in other breeds. This disorder is considered to be analogous to Duchenne muscular dystrophy in humans. Muscle tissues from affected dogs have reduced levels of dystrophin-associated proteins. Affected dogs show signs by eight to ten weeks of age, which include general muscle weakness, crouched posture, shuffling gait, splayed feet, and swallowing and chewing difficulty. The condition worsens rapidly between three and six months of age and is ultimately fatal. Gene therapies may one day be available for treatment.

GRMD is X-linked (sex-linked), meaning it is carried on the X chromosome. This means that males, with one X and one Y chromosome, will be affected if they inherit one X chromosome with the defective gene, whereas females (XX) would need to inherit the defective gene from both parents in order to be affected, which is rather unlikely. Thus, most affected dogs are males, although females can be carriers. Genetic tests can now identify dogs as clear, carriers, or affected.

*Your Golden's health and happiness are the products of both his genes and environment. Shared outdoor activity is a great health and spirit booster for dog and human.*

# Epilepsy

Seizures are not uncommon in dogs, and may or may not have hereditary causes. Many environmental causes can contribute to seizures, and very often the cause is never determined. Epilepsy is usually diagnosed when a dog, especially a young dog, has repeated seizures for no apparent reason. Such dogs very likely have a hereditary form of epilepsy, and should not be bred.

Dogs with recurrent seizures can be treated with phenobarbital. Dogs with only occasional seizures should probably be left untreated, however, as phenobarbital can somewhat decrease a dog's quality of life.

### Dealing with a Seizure

Convulsions typically begin with the dog acting nervous, and then increasingly peculiar, such as trembling, unresponsiveness, staring into space, and salivating profusely. This "pre-ictal" stage is followed by the ictal stage, in which the dog will typically stiffen, fall over, paddle its legs, and champ its jaws. The ictal stage usually lasts only a couple of minutes; if it continues for more than ten minutes you must get the dog to the emergency clinic.

• Remove other dogs from the area, as they often attack a convulsing dog.
• Wrap the dog securely in a blanket to prevent it from injuring itself on furniture or stairs.
• Never put your hands (or anything) in a convulsing dog's mouth.

**GOLD NUGGET**

**The Noblest Gift**
One of the noblest tributes to a Golden lost because of a hereditary problem is to donate in his or her memory to health research through the Golden Retriever Foundation, Rt. 2, Box 309, Jones, OK 73049 (http://www.grca.org/acquiring.htm#foundation). Even nobler, but more difficult, is to allow your Golden's disease to be studied by researchers trying to understand it by donating the affected organs.

After the ictal stage, the dog will remain disoriented, may be blind, and will pant and sleep. Your dog should be examined by your veterinarian as soon as possible. Take careful note of all characteristics and sequences of seizure activity to help diagnose a cause. For more information visit the Canine Epilepsy Resource Center at http://www.rt66.com/~dalcrazy/Epil-K9.html.

For a breed of such popularity, Goldens have surprisingly few widespread hereditary problems. With careful testing and responsible breeding, that number could become even lower. Meanwhile owners must be on the lookout for signs of and new treatments for these problems, and like all dog owners, make the very best of the far too short time we all have to share with our best friends.

## Chapter Eight

# Good as Gold

Golden Retrievers are famous for their intellectual and obedience feats, but this fame has sometimes created unfair expectations from new owners. Goldens aren't born trained, and even a Golden can't train itself. Yet some new owners, expecting a canine Einstein, believe their disobedient Golden is substandard and must either be unusually dumb or stubborn, when, in fact, the blame lies in improper training.

One reason Goldens are so successful in obedience competition is because they are high-energy dogs, a necessity in the hunt for high scores. High energy plus high intelligence equals a lot of imaginative activity. An imaginative Golden may seem disobedient at first, but chances are your dog is just trying to understand the rules of this new game called training.

## The Training Game

What do the best obedience, drug detection, show, and field Goldens have in common when they're on the

*Goldens love to show off their genius.*

job? Their tails are wagging. They are enjoying every minute because the activity has been made fun. Their attitude didn't come about because they were forced and punished into compliance. It came about because their trainers knew how to make training into a game. Sometimes the game may be challenging, but it is always winnable.

Just like people, Goldens may go through the motions of a job they are forced to do, but they will never do it well unless it's fun. Old-fashioned dog-training methods based on force are difficult, ineffective, and no fun for either dog or trainer. Punishment may tell a dog what *not* to do, but it can't tell a dog what it *should* do, and it can't make a dog *want* to do it. Rewards tell a dog what it should do, and make it want to do it. Praise, petting, food, and retrieving are all rewards for Goldens.

### Food as Reward

Professional animal trainers and animal learning scientists have shown that food training is highly effective. Food is used initially to guide the dog and later as a reward. The dog is then gradually weaned from getting a food reward for each correct response but, instead, is rewarded only at random correct responses. This random payoff is the same psychology used—very effectively—to induce people to put money (the correct response) into slot machines.

## Clicker Training

Professional dog trainers go one step further. They use a signal, such as a click sound, to instantly tell the dog when it has performed correctly. The signal is then followed by a food reward. A clicker signal is used because it is fast, noticeable, and something the dog otherwise does not encounter in everyday life. In order to apply this technique to the following instructions, whenever giving a reward is mentioned, you should precede it with a clicker signal. Even if you don't use a clicker,

---

*G O L D   N U G G E T*

### Equipment

The secret of training is not in the tools; it's in the trainer. Still, having the right tools can make things go a bit easier. Basic training equipment usually includes a short (6 foot [1.8 m]) lead, a long (about 20 foot [6 m]) lightweight lead, and a collar. Traditionally, a choke collar has been used, but many trainers prefer a buckle collar, and some are finding the halter-type collars to be best for some Goldens.

---

always precede any tangible reward with "*Good!*" and praise.

## Timing

Great dog trainers have great timing. The crux of training is anticipation: A dog comes to anticipate that after hearing a command, it will be rewarded if it performs some action, and it will eventually perform this action without further assistance from you. Your timing is everything; remember this sequence:

**1. Name.** Alert your dog that your next words are directed toward her by preceding commands with her name.

**2. Command.** Always give the command with the same word, in the same tone.

**3. Action.** Don't simultaneously place the dog into position as you say the command, which negates the predictive value of the command.

**4. Reward.** As soon as possible after the dog has performed correctly, give the signal, "*Good!*" followed by a reward.

The sooner a reward follows an action, the better the association. It's sometimes difficult to reward a dog instantly, however, so you can do the next best thing by immediately signaling the dog a reward is coming. The best way to do this is with a noticeable sound the dog otherwise doesn't hear in everyday life, such as that from a clicker. The next best thing is simply to say "*Good!*" In either case, give the signal just after the action and before the reward.

# Basic Training

It's never too early or too late to start the education of your Golden. With a very young pup, train for even shorter time periods than you would an adult. By the time your Golden reaches six months of age, she should know how to *sit*, *down*, *stay*, *come*, and *heel*. These exercises will be demonstrated with the help of a budding genius named Sissy.

First, you have to get Sissy's attention. Say "*Sissy, watch me*," and when she looks in your direction, say "*Good!*" and give her a treat or other reward. Gradually require Sissy to look at you for longer and longer periods before rewarding her.

## Come

If Sissy learns only one command, that command should be to come when called; it could save her life. She probably already knows how to come; after all, she comes when she's called for dinner. You want her to respond to "*Sissy, come*" with that same enthusiasm; in other words, "*Come*" should always be associated with good things. Never have your dog come to you and then scold her for something she has done; in her mind, she is being scolded for coming, not for any earlier misdeed. Nor should you call your dog to you at the end of an off-lead walk. You don't want her to associate coming to you with relinquishing her freedom. Call her to you several times during the walk, reward and praise her, and then send her back out to play. This could be a special treat, a chance to retrieve, or even the chance to chase after you. To train to come:

**1.** Have a helper gently restrain Sissy while you back away and entice her until she is struggling to get to you. Then excitedly call "*Sissy, come!*" and turn and run away. Your helper should immediately release her. When she catches you, give her a special reward. Always keep up a jolly attitude and make her feel lucky to be part of such a wonderful game.

**2.** Next, place Sissy on lead, call "*Sissy, come!*" and quickly run away. If she ignores you for more

---

*G O L D   N U G G E T*

### Slip Collars

A choke collar is not for choking! In fact, it is more correctly termed a slip collar. The proper way to administer a correction with a choke collar is with a *very* gentle snap, then immediate release. The choke collar is placed on the dog so that the ring with the lead attached comes up around the left side of the dog's neck, and through the other ring. If put on backwards, it will not release itself after being tightened, since you will be on the right side of your dog for most training. Never leave a choke collar on a dog! See page 100 for more information about collar choices.

*An obedient Golden is a trustworthy companion in public.*

than a second, tug on the lead to get her attention, but don't drag her to you. After the tug, be sure to run backwards and make her think it was all part of the game.

---

## GOLD NUGGET

### Training Platforms

Teach stationary exercises, such as "*sit*," "*down*," and "*stay*," on a raised surface. This allows you to have eye contact with your dog and gives you a better vantage point from which to help your dog learn. It also helps keep your pet from being distracted and taking off to play.

---

**3.** Then place her on a longer line, allow her to meander about, and in the midst of her investigations, call, run backwards, and reward. After a few repetitions, drop the long line, let her mosey around a bit, then call. If she begins to come, run away and let her chase you as part of the game. If she doesn't come, pick up the line and give a tug, then run away as usual.

As Sissy becomes more reliable, you should begin to practice—still on the long line—in the presence of distractions. Hold onto her leash just in case the distractions prove too enticing.

Some dogs develop a habit of dancing around just out of your reach, considering your futile grabs to be another part of this wonderful game. You can prevent this by requiring Sissy to allow you to hold her by the collar before you reward her. Eventually, you may add sitting in front of you as part of the game. Note that dogs in obedience trials are expected to sit in front upon returning, whereas dogs in field trials are usually expected to circle behind and sit in *heel* position upon returning.

This may seem like a lot of work to teach a simple command that your dog can almost teach herself, but it will save you a lot of wasted time in the long run, and perhaps a lot of grief. Besides, it should be fun, not work!

## Sit

"*Sit*" is the prototypical dog command, and with good reason. It's a simple way to control your dog and it's easy.

**1.** The simplest way to teach the *sit* is to stand in front of your pup and hold a tidbit just above her eye level.

**2.** Say "*Sissy, sit,*" and then move the tidbit toward her until it's slightly behind and above her eyes. You may have to keep a hand on her rump to prevent her from jumping up.

**3.** When she begins to look up and bend her hind legs, say "*Good!*" then offer the tidbit.

**4.** Repeat this, requiring her to bend her legs more and more until she must be sitting before receiving the "*Good!*" and reward. If she backs up instead of sitting down, place her rear against a wall while training.

## Stay

A dangerous habit of many dogs is to bolt through open doors. Teach your dog to sit and stay until given the release signal before walking through the front door or exiting your car.

**1.** Have Sissy sit, then say "*Stay*" in a soothing voice—if you precede a command with the dog's name, the dog will have a tendency to jump up in anticipation. If she tries to get up or lie down, gently but instantly place her back into position. Work up to a few seconds, give a release word— "*OK!*"—then praise and reward.

**2.** Next, step out, starting with your right foot, and turn to stand directly in front of your dog while she stays. It's tempting to stare into your dog's eyes as if hypnotizing her to stay, but this really will have the opposite effect. Staring is perceived by the dog as a threat and can be intimidating, causing the dog to squirm out of position and come to you, her leader.

**3.** Work up to longer times, but don't ask a young puppy to stay longer than 30 seconds. The object is not to push your dog to the limit, but to let her succeed.

**4.** Finally, practice with the dog on lead by the front door or in the car. For a reward, take your dog for a walk.

## Down

When you need your Golden to stay in one place for a long time you

*The Golden is a master of precision heeling, as shown in this perfect demonstration of heel position.*

can't expect her to sit or stand. This is when the *down* command really comes in handy.

**1.** Begin teaching the *down* command with the dog in the sitting position. Say "*Sissy, down*," then show her a tidbit and move it below her nose toward the ground. If she reaches down to get it, give it to her.

**2.** Repeat, requiring her to reach farther down, without lifting her rear from the ground, until she has to lower her elbows to the ground. Never try to cram her into the *down* position, which can scare a submissive dog and cause a dominant dog to resist.

**3.** Practice the *down/stay* just as you did the *sit/stay*.

### Heel

A pup's first experience walking on leash should be positive. Never drag a reluctant pup or let her hit the end of the lead. Start by coaxing her a few steps at a time with food. When she follows you, praise and reward. In this way she begins to realize that following you while walking on lead pays off.

Once your pup is prancing alongside you, it's time to ask a little more of her. Even if you have no intention of teaching a perfect competition

---

## GOLD NUGGET

### Starting Off on the Right Foot (or Left)

By stepping off with your right foot when you want your dog to *stay*, and your left foot when your want your dog to *heel*, you will give your dog an eye-level cue about what you are saying.

---

*heel*, your dog should know how to walk politely at your side.

**1.** Have Sissy sit in *heel* position: on your left side with her neck next to and parallel with your leg. If you line up your feet and your dog's front feet, that's close enough.

**2.** Say "*Sissy, heel*," and step off with your left foot first. During your first few practice sessions keep her on a short lead, holding her in *heel* position, and of course praising her. The traditional method of letting her lunge to the end of the lead and then snapping her back is unfair if you haven't first shown her what you expect. Instead, after a few sessions of showing her *heel* position, give her a little more loose lead and use a tidbit to guide her into correct position.

**3.** If your Golden still forges ahead after you have shown her what is expected, pull her back to position with a quick gentle tug, then release, of the lead. If, after a few days of practice, she still seems oblivious to your efforts, then turn unexpectedly several times; teach her that it's her responsibility to keep an eye on you.

**4.** Keep up a pace that requires your dog to walk fairly briskly; too slow a pace gives her time to sniff and sightsee; a brisk pace will focus her attention upon you. Add some about-faces and right and left turns, and walk at different speeds. Teach her to sit every time you stop.

**5.** Vary your routine to combat boredom. Be sure to give the "*OK*" command before allowing her to sniff, forge, and meander on lead.

# Higher Aspirations

If you think obedience titles may be in your future, you might as well think big—after all, you have a Golden Retriever! The exercises for advanced titles are not only a lot tougher, but much more fun. Two of the basic components of higher obedience exercises are retrieving and jumping, both naturals for Goldens. Many trainers find the best time to teach the advanced exercises is in the beginning. So rather than wait until your dog has earned the Novice degree, you may wish to introduce retrieving and jumping now.

Unlike field work, your dog will be retrieving dumbbells and gloves in obedience trials, not birds and dummies. You should introduce your Golden to these items when she is still young, but they should not be used as toys. Your dog needs to know that when you ask her to retrieve a dumbbell or glove, as fun as it might be, you are serious and it's not an optional game. You may not be able to rely on your Golden retrieving reliably amidst all

---

*G O L D   N U G G E T*

**Circus Clowns**

Many people believe the story that Goldens are descended from Russian circus dogs *must* be true; after all, how else would you get a dog that could learn so many tricks and be such a clown at the same time?

*Jumping can add excitement to training, but it's best to build up gradually so that dogs learn correct jumping form.*

the distractions of an obedience trial unless your dog has learned the force-fetch (see page 117).

## Jumping

Several advanced exercises require high and broad jumping. Goldens are fairly heavy-bodied dogs, and years of repeated jumping can be stressful on heavy dogs' joints. In fact, many great obedience Goldens have had to retire prematurely from competition because they could no longer withstand the stress of jumping. Besides keeping your obedience prospect trim and healthy, you can teach proper jumping style by giving your dog plenty of opportunity to jump low—and only low—jumps when she's younger. Only when she matures can you

introduce slightly higher jumps. When she begins to seriously practice advanced exercise, vary the jump height so that your dog learns to judge height before jumping, but do most of your practicing over low jumps so you don't stress her joints.

## Hand Signals

Even more advanced exercises will involve hand signals and scent discrimination. Again, there is no reason to postpone introducing these concepts to your dog. Teach hand signals just as you would voice signals; if your dog already knows voice signals, add hand signals by immediately preceding your standard voice command with a signal. If you plan to show your dog in field competition make sure your field and obedience signals don't conflict with one another.

## Scent Discrimination

For scent discrimination, get your dog accustomed to using her nose to find hidden objects with your scent on them. Throw a scented object in the midst of several unscented objects that are tied down. Your dog will learn that the articles without your scent can't be picked up. Be careful you don't contaminate the other objects with your scent by touching them.

## Tricks

Many Goldens find the basic obedience exercises boring, so teaching advanced exercises along with basic ones can help keep your Golden's enthusiasm high. Another way to keep up enthusiasm is with fun dog tricks. Tricks are easy to teach with the help of the same obedience concepts outlined in the training section. Try these standards:

• Teach "roll over" by telling your dog to lie down, and then saying "*Roll over*," and luring her over on her side with a treat. Once she is reliably rolling on her side, use the treat to guide her onto her back. Then guide her the rest of the way, eventually giving the treat only when she has rolled all the way over.

• Teach "catch" by tossing a tidbit or ball in a high arc over your dog's face. If she misses, snatch the tidbit off the ground before she can reach it. Eventually, she'll realize that to beat you to the bounty, she'll have

to grab it before it reaches the ground.

• Teach "shake hands" by having your dog sit. Say "*Shake*" and hold a treat in your closed hand in front of your dog. Many dogs will pick up a foot to paw at your hand; these are the naturals. With others, you have to give a little nudge on the leg, or lure the dog's head far to one side so she has to lift the leg up on the opposite side. As soon as the paw leaves the ground, reward! Then require the dog to lift it higher and longer.

• Teach "speak" by saying "*Speak*" when it appears your Golden is about to bark. Then reward. Don't reward barking unless you've first said "*Speak*."

# The Canine Good Citizen

Half the fun of owning a Golden Retriever is showing her off in public and including her in outdoor adventures. Half the problem of owning such a dog is that you attract atten-

G O L D ★ S T A R

The incomparable Golden "Air Bud" parlayed a talent for sinking baskets into a series of movies in which he, and his successors, displayed their abilities to win ball games and hearts.

tion wherever you go. People will stop to ask about your dog and will not be able to resist petting her. While this can be a great deal of fun and a wonderful way to meet people, it won't be much fun if your dog is barking or jumping all over everyone she meets, and it will be a bad reflection on the Golden Retriever breed.

In order to recognize formally dogs that behave in public, the AKC offers the Canine Good Citizen (CGC) certificate, which requires your Golden to:
• Accept a friendly stranger who greets you.
• Sit politely for petting by a stranger.
• Allow a stranger to pet and groom her.
• Walk politely on a loose lead.
• Walk through a crowd on a lead.
• Sit and lie down on command and stay in place while on a 20-foot (6 m) line.
• Calm down after play.
• React politely to another dog. React calmly to distractions.
• Remain calm when tied for three minutes in the owner's absence, under supervision by a stranger.

**Remember:** The most magnificent champion in the show or obedience ring is no credit to its breed if it is not a good public citizen in the real world.

*Trained dogs make pleasurable companions, but even the best-trained dogs can have lapses. Always use a leash in any situation that could present unpredictable temptations.*

# Obedience Classes

Good obedience classes are great aids for training your dog to behave properly at home, in public, and in competition. To find a good class, get referrals from other Golden trainers and sit in on the class. If the class uses outdated yank-and-jerk methods, look elsewhere; your friend's well-being is worth too much.

If you plan to go on to compete in obedience, a class is a necessity. Obedience trials are held amidst great distractions. It would be nearly impossible for your dog to pass without having some experience working around other dogs. Obedience classes are filled with people who share many of your same interests. If you take the plunge into competition, class is a place to celebrate wins and laugh about failures.

Sometimes your Golden will be the star pupil; other times you will feel like the class dunce. If you have a particularly unruly dog, you may gauge your progress by simply being able to have your dog stand calmly beside you at the end of the course. Each dog will progress at its own pace; every dog will improve, and many dogs will profit from repeating the same class after using the first time through as a warm-up.

Obedience classes train you to train your dog. Don't let your dog down. Remember, there's no such thing as an untrainable dog, only untrained dogs—and whose fault is that?

**GOLD NUGGET**

## Golden Rules
• *Guide, don't force.* Goldens already want to please you; your job is to simply show them the way. Forcing them can distract or intimidate them, actually slowing down learning.
• *Once is enough.* Repeating a command over and over, or shouting it louder and louder, never helped anyone understand what is expected of them. Your Golden is not hard of hearing.
• *Give your dog a hunger for learning.* Your Golden will work better if her stomach is not full, and she will be more responsive to food rewards. Never try to train a sleepy, tired, or hot dog.
• *Be a quitter.* You, and your dog, have good days and bad days. On bad days, quit. Never train your dog when you are irritable or impatient. Even on good days, don't push it. After about 15 minutes, your dog's performance will begin to suffer unless a lot of play is involved. Keep your Golden wanting more, and you will have a happy, willing obedience partner.
• *The best-laid plans don't include dogs.* Nothing ever goes as perfectly as it does in training instructions. Although there may be setbacks, you can train your dog, as long as you remember to be consistent, firm, gentle, realistic, patient—and have a very good sense of humor.

# Chapter Nine

# The Golden Retriever Afield

Golden owners who love sharing good splashing adventures and quiet solitude with their Goldens often find that taking them into the field is the most rewarding activity of all. Golden Retrievers have the ability to approach even the hardest jobs with an incomparable enthusiasm, a trait never more evident than when they are in the field and faced with a challenging retrieve. All Goldens are born with a certain amount of hunting ability—some more than others—but they can't hone it to perfection without training. Developing a good hunting retriever will take some hard work and a good dog. Developing a competitive field trial retriever will take tremendous work and a spectacular dog.

## The Hunting Retriever

Any Golden can retrieve, but that's child's play for a real hunting partner. A top hunting retriever must

mark unerringly the fall of shot birds, follow the handler's directions to hidden birds, and trail and brave escaping and uncooperative wounded birds. It must push through deep cover, plunge into icy water, and swim against strong currents. It must be fast, strong, and tireless, biddable yet self-assured, and with natural bird sense and persistence.

Don't think that just because your Golden is a "natural-born retriever" you can merely turn him loose in the field and have a good hunting partner. While a natural-born retriever may get the job done as long as everything goes perfectly, it's the other 90 percent of the time that you need a well-trained, natural-born retriever. An untrained dog cannot be turned away from potentially dangerous situations, including decoy lines that could potentially entangle and drown him, or back from swimming out to sea after he has overshot a fallen duck. An untrained dog doesn't hold still in a boat or blind, and can jostle the hunter just as the hunter makes a shot, overturn a boat, or rush out and steal another

*Retrieving birds is the Golden's reason for being.*

**111**

GOLD NUGGET

**Professional Help**
Contact the Professional Retriever Trainers Association for a list of professional trainers. The PRTA is at N4372 22nd Lane, Montello, WI 53949, tel: (414) 295-6834; http://starsouth.com/prta/members.htm.

dog's bird. An untrained dog rushes out after the first bird is shot, missing the fall of subsequent birds or scaring them away. An untrained dog can't reliably find or retrieve wounded birds, allowing them to escape to die a slow death. An untrained dog can't be directed to a bird that has fallen out of the dog's view, wasting a natural resource.

Don't rely only on natural instincts if you want a good retrieving partner, but don't rely only on training either if you want an exceptional partner. Some Goldens are more naturally inclined than others, and if a hunting retriever is your top priority, you will do best to get your Golden from a hunting background (see page 28). Keep in mind that not all field titles are equal; some require much more ability than others.

## Training Resources

Many people who want a top-notch field dog have neither the time nor experience to train their dog themselves. Professional retriever trainers can teach your dog basic to advanced retrieving skills. This will take at least a couple of months for the most basic skills, to a couple of years for competition-quality skills. If your main goal is to have a field trial contender, you should use a professional trainer, at least at first. Not all trainers are created equal, so you need to be very careful you choose a reputable one who uses humane methods and has safe facilities. Attend several field trials and watch how competing trainers treat their dogs, how the dogs act, and how the retriever community regards them.

Of course, it's more fun to train your dog yourself. If you decide to give training a try, you should still join a local training or practice group. If

*Hunting with a capable dog makes a day in the field a pleasure whether birds are bagged or not.*

you are fortunate enough to live near a professional, volunteer as a helper and thrower, and keep your eyes and mind open. You should also consult several books and videotapes about training retrievers (see page 193–195); many different techniques exist, and some may work better with different dogs. As in any endeavor that entails a high level of performance, there is no one way to train a retriever. The information presented in this chapter represents only a sampling of training techniques. Dogs always complicate matters by not responding like machines, so rest assured that even the best trainers with the best dogs often have to backtrack and rethink their methods for every individual dog. That's part of the challenge that keeps advanced trainers always looking forward to the next dog; but it's also part of the reason that trying to train a dog from a book is often so frustrating—unfortunately, the dogs never read the same book as the trainers. Whether you choose to do it yourself, hire a professional, or just watch from afar, you should be aware of some of the steps that go into the making of a field dog.

## First Steps

Don't be discouraged if your dog doesn't retrieve, swim, or otherwise perform retrieverly feats at a young age. All dogs mature and progress at different rates, but our star pupil will be a gifted pup named Max. The best time to start training Max is as

*The best time to start field training is when your pup is young.*

soon as he responds to you and shows a desire to retrieve. Encourage retrieving and carrying by throwing items, such as stuffed socks, and later soft paint rollers and bird wings, a short distance, then calling Max to you. Kneeling or bending usually encourages pups to come, as does running in the opposite direction. Never chase, which encourages keep-away rather than retrieving. If Max won't come, either attach a lightweight line or try again in more confined space with fewer distractions; a hallway is ideal. When he brings the object to you, praise him enthusiastically, let him hold it for a little while, and then give a command word, such as *"Give"* or *"Out,"* for

GOLD NUGGET

## Training Equipment Checklist

- Flat-buckle collar
- Leash—brightly colored so you can find it after dropping it in long grass or mud
- Check cord—thin nylon cord, 1 to 3 feet (30 to 91 cm) long, that can be snapped to or strung around the dog's collar
- Whistle to be worn around the neck; one made especially for retriever training is best.
- Plastic bumpers, or dummies, both white and black for marking; orange for blind retrieves.

   Attach about a 1-foot (30 cm) rope to one end by threading it through the eyelet and knotting both ends of the rope; use this throwing rope to increase your throw distance.
- Duck call, to accustom your dog to the sound of ducks and attract the dog's attention when used by an assistant.
- Blank gun
- Decoys
- Birds, either frozen or live; check with your local Fish and Game Department to see if you need a dog training permit for birds.
- White cones for advanced work; get three or four.

him to let go. Don't grab the item or do anything to encourage Max to hold on tight; you want to gently persuade him to give it to you. Follow

with praise and a reward, such as throwing the item again. Don't throw it more than three or four times each session, though; you want your pup to quit while still wanting more, and never to associate retrieving with getting tired. At this stage, Max can do no wrong, only some things more right than others. Keep it a game!

**A word of caution:** Sometimes, the natural-born retriever's desire to carry items is in conflict with what we consider to be proper housedog etiquette. You can't expect to reprimand a young pup for carrying around your shoes and socks in the house, and then praise him for carrying around similar items in the yard, without creating a lot of confusion. You can teach your dog to discriminate the right items from the wrong items later; for now, just be sure the wrong items are never available. This means that even if the rest of the family is not actively involved in training, they must know to keep their belongings out of puppy reach and never to scold or chase the pup if he does carry their belongings.

**Early marking:** A good retriever does a lot more than hold things. A retriever that cannot mark, that is, watch and remember the fall of the bird and get to that spot, isn't very useful in the field. A dog that has to be directed to every bird, or that relies on running around in the general vicinity until it stumbles across a bird, is a nuisance in the field and a nonqualifier at a hunting test. Some dogs seem to have greater inborn marking ability than others, but any dog can have its ability enhanced through training. Start easy, by letting Max follow short throws with easily visible falls. You want him to rely on his vision at this stage, rather than his nose.

As Max gets a little older and more proficient, you can start to challenge him a little more. Go for walks and bring a ball or training dummy. Use objects that contrast with the color of the ground, remembering that dogs are red-green color-blind. Solid white or black objects are ideal. Throw the object in the open, in cover, over logs or streams. You want Max to dash after it; if not, you may wish to build his speed by racing him to the prize. This, however, is seldom a problem, unless you overdo it. As before, less is better; keep Max thinking of each retrieve as a special treat. You want

him to race out to the object, scoop it up, and race back to you with it. A tired pup will learn to conserve energy by loping out, then dawdling over the object while he catches his breath, and then loping back to you or not returning at all. Don't use retrieving to condition your dog; you might build up his stamina, but you might also tear down his enthusiasm.

## Water Work

Your dog will often be retrieving through water. Although this is usually no problem for a Golden, you can help to make sure Max dog is as at home in the water as on land by providing a child's wading pool for early practice. Fill the pool with a little more water each day, and encourage him to play in it. If you let Max

*In his element...*

run until he's hot first, he'll especially relish the opportunity to jump right in. Cold weather can be a problem for training young pups to swim. Don't ask your pup to enter cold water. It's unpleasant and bad training.

**Swimming:** Max will need to graduate from wading and splashing to swimming. This is best done with water that naturally slopes from shallow to deeper depths, and also best done if you go into the water with him. Never throw Max into the water with a sink-or-swim mentality; you will not encourage confidence that way. Swimming is natural for your Golden, but even a Golden needs practice. Most dogs think they can walk on water and their first swimming efforts are unsuccessful because they are trying to lift their front feet too high. You can help by holding the rear end up and preventing the front feet from splashing. Even without your help, your dog will catch on.

Don't expect Max to retrieve while swimming yet; he needs to concentrate on one thing at a time. You can throw items into shallow water so he learns how to scoop them out while they're floating. Only when he gets more confident in the water should you introduce short retrieves. Later, encourage him to rush into the water, and introduce higher bank entries, but always check first for underwater hazards that could injure, or even impale, a diving dog. Don't push a youngster into such feats until he is confident in doing them.

**Boats:** Max should eventually be introduced to riding quietly in a duck boat, and jumping from it into the water on (and only on) command. Getting him back into the boat can be tricky, so make sure your first attempts are not so far from land that he (and you!) couldn't swim to safety. You never want to frighten Max by letting him think he's stranded in the water. If you're strong, you can lift him in, or you can help by pushing down on his head once he's placed his front feet on the boat. Some hunters attach a little floating ramp to the boat to help the dog get in. Full-fledged swimming and boating lessons are for older puppies; you still have plenty of preliminary work to do with your youngster.

# Field Obedience

Max will need to learn some basic obedience. The most talented retriever in the world is useless if he runs amok and ignores his handler in the field. Start with the basics: *Sit, stay, come,* and *heel* (see page 101). Eventually, Max will need to know how to sit and stay to await your command to retrieve when a dummy is thrown or bird is downed. *Heeling* and *coming* are also vital lessons for a retrieving dog. An important aspect of *heeling* is the ability to sit in perfectly straight alignment in *heel* position. A dog trained to sit precisely at *heel* can be positioned facing the direction in which he is to be sent on a blind retrieve. Teach Max to adjust his position when you turn a few degrees on your heel. Make it a game, and for now don't let absolute obedience or precision get in the way of having fun. This is one of many skills that takes time to develop.

**The whistle:** You'll also want to introduce the whistle, which is a much better way to give commands at a distance than shouting into the wind. A series of three to four short staccato tweets is customarily used to call the dog, and one sharp tweet to stop him. Train to the whistle by tweeting it just before the verbal command you usually use; soon Max will anticipate the command according to the whistle. There's no reason Max can't learn whistle commands as easily, if not more easily, than voice commands.

# Force-fetching

Most serious retriever trainers advocate force-fetching, in which the dog is trained to retrieve on command in order to avoid an unpleasant but brief pinch to his ear. There's a reason for this: Despite the fact the dog may love to retrieve, unless his retrieval is under the handler's absolute control, the dog is the one in control. A dog that retrieves only when he feels like it may refuse a difficult retrieve because it's not fun. The very fact that retrieving is normally so instinctive and fun has prevented the dog from realizing that it's more than a game; it's a duty and a command. A dog that has been taught to retrieve on command knows he's there to do a job, not to satisfy his own whims. Done correctly, the force-fetch is not cruel, partly because the dog learns the concept very quickly. For this reason, it's best to have an experienced trainer show you how to do the force-fetch correctly. Finally, consider your goals for your dog. If you don't need an absolutely reliable hunting companion or competitor, you can probably get along just fine without a force-trained dog. You will almost certainly need to employ force-training if you intend to go on to field trial competition, however. Not all trainers use the force method, just most of the successful ones.

The force-fetch is taught to older youngsters, after they are retrieving for fun and know some basic obedience. It consists of two training phases: first the hold, then the fetch. The basic steps are as follows:

### The Hold

**1.** Have Max sit, wearing a leash and collar. By standing on the leash, you will have both hands free.

**2.** Place a dummy in Max's mouth. If he doesn't take the dummy willingly, push the dummy against his front teeth and press his lips against one side of his mouth until he opens his mouth.

**3.** Command "*Hold.*" By tipping Max's head slightly backwards and stroking him under the chin, you can prevent him from spitting out the dummy. Praise Max for holding. Later you can gently tap him under the chin if he tries to drop the dummy.

**4.** Give a release command, such as "*Give*" or "*Out*," and take the dummy. Praise. Work up to longer times.

**5.** After Max holds the dummy while sitting, practice with him holding it while heeling and sitting.

**6.** Only after Max is holding and carrying reliably, should you ask him to take the dummy voluntarily, or fetch.

### The Fetch

**1.** Have Max sit, wearing a leash and collar.

**2.** Place one hand under the collar, which should be snug up behind Max's ears, and place the thumb and index finger on either side of one of his ears, in a pinching position. You can also use the collar to pinch against.

**3.** Hold the dummy against Max's front teeth, command "*Fetch*," and pinch his ear until he opens his mouth, at which point quickly slide the dummy in his mouth and immediately stop pinching. Timing is vital. Be sure to praise him when he takes the dummy.

**4.** Have Max hold, then release, the dummy on command.

**5.** With only a few repetitions, Max learns that taking the dummy relieves the pinching.

**6.** Gradually increase the distance Max needs to reach for the dummy. He will reach quickly for it in order to avoid the pinch.

**7.** The transition of reaching for the dummy from your hand to reaching for it from the ground can be difficult. Do it gradually, with only one end of the dummy touching the ground at first.

**8.** Gradually increase the distance at which the dummy is placed or thrown on the ground. If Max refuses, you must quickly remind him with an ear pinch.

Strangely enough, most dogs are actually more eager retrievers after being force-trained. Most trainers seldom have to repeat the lessons, except in cases in which dogs decide the retrieve is too difficult; then they get a reminder that they must retrieve not only because it is fun to do, but also because it is your wish and their job.

# Beginning Retrieving

When Max is retrieving enthusiastically, ask a helper to act as a thrower. The thrower should stand 10 to 15 feet (3 to 4.6 m) ahead and to the side of you. He or she should say something (commonly "*Hup, hup*") to get Max's attention, and then toss the object. Let Max retrieve it and encourage him to bring the object back to you, not to the thrower.

Keep throws short; you want to keep your pup's energy and enthusiasm high. Increase interest and challenge by throwing over different terrain, across little ditches or wide puddles. Some dogs tend to run at the thrower. If this happens, move the thrower in closer to you and have

*Retrieving-dummies are almost as much fun as real birds.*

the thrower increase the throw distance. You can also add a third person to stand between you and the thrower; this accustoms the dog to the idea that it should not focus on running to any person in the field, but on marking the object.

Once Max is hurtling after thrown dummies, it's time to introduce restraint as part of the game. He should already understand the *sit* and *stay* commands, but for insurance, take hold of his collar. Wait for the dummy to just barely hit the ground before releasing and giving the signal to fetch; often, just the dog's name is used. If Max tries to go after the dummy before being sent, don't reprimand him; just restrain him. It will no doubt take several tries, but you must always be careful not to let him get away with breaking even once. You can keep him on a slip cord (which is a piece of line looped through the ring of his collar in such a way that when you release one end of the line, it can slip through the ring), and release it only when you give the command to retrieve. Even after that, it's helpful to have a friend who can scoop up the dummy if Max breaks before you have a chance to restrain him. This is even more critical when using birds. Max needs to know that rushing ahead will only postpone the opportunity to retrieve.

# Birds

Dummies are great for everyday training, but Goldens weren't bred to retrieve dummies; they were bred to retrieve birds, and all kinds of birds. You may have already been using a bird wing for one of your retrieving items. The next step is an actual bird—but one that is already dead. Although freshly killed is best, you can also freeze dead birds complete with feathers or, if you're lucky, get frozen birds from hunting clubs or other sources. Check with other trainers in your area. Birds should be frozen with their wings folded tight to their bodies. Be sure to thaw them partially before using. A fully frozen bird isn't birdy-smelling enough to give Max the proper idea of what's going on, but a fully thawed bird is too temptingly soft and easy to bite. A partially thawed bird has a frozen core that is resistant and unappealing to bite into. Start with smaller birds, such as pigeons, and gradually move up to larger ones.

A bird is a much more enticing item than a dummy, and Max may take his time with it, mouthing and sniffing in order to get the full effect. This is only natural, and as long as you encourage him to bring the bird in, all is going as planned. Sometimes a dog continues to bite down hard on the bird. Some trainers sug-

*A good retrieve is performed with speed, style, and accuracy.*

gest remedial lessons with a bristle or wire brush to teach the dog to carry items more gingerly, but the lesson may not transfer to birds, especially if your dog has already made it a habit.

Max may also race around the yard with a bird, or drop it before getting it all the way to you. Neither is acceptable behavior, but both can be worked on by running backwards and calling him to you. Even a dog that has dropped the bird will usually pick it up before he runs after you. The dog that drops the bird at your feet rather than delivering it to your hands is treated in a like manner. Eventually, you will want your dog to sit in front of or beside you; as a sitting dog looks up at you, the bird naturally falls back into his mouth and is less likely to be dropped. Retrieving to hand not only looks good, but a duck dropped in the water can drift away and a dropped crippled bird can run away.

Max may be so enthralled with a bird that he refuses to relinquish it to you. If you grab and pull the bird, you have just entered into a fun game of tug-o-war (and very likely pulled the bird in two); if you reprimand Max, you have taught him to stay away from you when he has a bird. If your dog won't relinquish birds go back to controlled training with a dummy and practice the release on command.

**Crippled birds:** If you plan to take Max hunting, unless you're the world's best sharpshooter, he'll need to know how to handle crip-

pled birds. Sometimes a cripple may take off running on land, and he'll need to trail it. Begin trailing training by dragging a dead bird for a short distance through heavy cover. Hold the bird away from your tracks by dangling it from a line hanging from a long stick. Start with trails of only a few feet and gradually work up.

Once Max finds a cripple, he will need to know how to hold it. The time to learn is not in the middle of the water with a fighting goose. In all fairness you should never put your dog in this position, and you should help your dog with a cripple whenever possible—but it's not always possible. You can help your dog be prepared by letting him retrieve live birds. Pigeons can have one wing tied so that they can flutter and run but not fly away. Max should still retrieve the bird without injuring it. Ducks can be shackled—in which their wings and feet are tied loosely—so they can swim and even flap in the water but not escape. It is important that if you hamper the ability of any bird to walk or fly you make absolutely sure it cannot escape, whereby it would experience a lingering death. It is also important that you employ as humane methods as possible. Do not reuse birds if they are injured. Never abuse birds.

## Decoys

Decoys are part of the duck-hunting experience, and a part you don't want Max to bring back to you. Max has been trained on inanimate dummies for much of his training, so it's natural for him to grab a decoy as just another training item. The easiest way to prevent this is to set out your decoys along with a real dead duck in shallow water. With Max on lead, wade among them and discourage Max every time he attempts to pick up a decoy. When he comes to the real duck, praise and let him retrieve it. Feathers are a lot more rewarding than plastic or wood, so your dog will quickly learn to search for the real McCoy, not the plastic decoy.

## Gunshots

Max should get used to loud noises; gun-shy retrievers are no help in the field! You don't need to fire a gun at first; just get him used to loud sudden noises. Follow each noise with a treat or a chance to retrieve. If Max shows any uneasiness, act jolly and convince him nothing is amiss. Don't coddle him for nervous behavior. If he remains nervous, back down a bit and try something not quite as loud. A nervous or gun-shy pup can be trained using the same techniques used to work with any noise phobia (page 161).

When Max is older, start introducing louder noises by having a helper shoot a .22 caliber blank pistol at a good distance from him, preferably downwind. Feed or throw something for him immediately after the shot. Later, have your helper move slightly closer—around 50 yards (46 m) from

you—and have the helper both shoot and then throw a dummy or bird. Your thrower should replace the *"Hup, hup"* attention command with a gunshot. Gradually work closer and increase the caliber of the gun; eventually, Max will associate a gunshot with a chance to retrieve. Some dogs will associate the gunshot so much that they will forget their restraint lessons and rush forward at the sound of the shot. This is an easy problem to deal with since the dog has usually bolted before the dummy or bird is thrown. Simply don't throw it and make the dog return for another try.

## Marking

Marking is one of the integral skills of a good retriever. It takes a good dog, a good trainer, and a lot of work. Don't expect to rush to or through these steps. Max should be an eager and reliable retriever before beginning serious marked retrieves.

Your thrower, or gun, should be positioned well in front of you and the dog, at varying distances. The thrower should already be in place when you walk Max onto the field; orient Max toward the thrower, have him sit, command him to mark, and when he is looking at the thrower have the thrower yell *"Hup, hup"* or shoot a blank, and immediately throw the object. The thrower should toss the dummies (or dead birds) at varying distances and angles, from 90 degrees to either side, to 45 degrees toward or away from you, to directly away or even directly toward you. Your goal at this stage is to make sure Max is marking the fall, not running toward the thrower. The thrower should vary locations, sometimes moving while you and the dog have temporarily left the field so that Max cannot see the thrower's movements. As before, gradually add various changes in terrain and levels of difficulty.

Work on single water marks, and add different entry angles and obstacles and lengthen the distance to the water entry. Do not set up any situations that tempt your dog to run along the shoreline, however. Your dog should enter the water directly and strongly. Eventually, you will add double water marks and triple land marks, but that is advanced work.

**Double marks:** Double marks are what separate the dogs from the pups. Double land marks are introduced when the dog is reliably returning from singles and can sit long enough to be sent again. If you have gotten to this stage, you are obviously a determined trainer, and probably have access to experienced advisers and helpers. Now is a good time to make use of them. If you don't, you can congratulate yourself on a job well done and tackle doubles as your next challenge. One way to do this is to divide your yard with temporary fencing. Stand at one end of and in line with the fence and throw two easy marks, one on each side of the fence. The fence prevents Max from picking up one dummy and

GOLD NUGGET

**Electronic Collars**
Because of the difficulty in communicating with a dog working at great distances from the handler, many handlers find electronic training collars to be helpful; however, they must be used with full understanding of the techniques involved.

then running directly to the other. Instead, he has to return to you before being sent for the second one. You can also use the corner of your house for this exercise. Send your dog for the second thrown object first, then for the first thrown object, which is the memory mark. By using a bird for the memory mark, you can encourage memory development and build enthusiasm.

# Blind Retrieves

Many good hunting retrievers can perform adequately relying on marking alone, as long as you resign yourself to the fact that you will eventually lose some birds. If this is not satisfactory to you, or if you intend to participate with your dog in trials or tests, you will need to learn to handle, or direct, your dog on blind retrieves (those falls out of the dog's sight). Again, this is advanced training and not expected of puppies or, for that matter, inexperienced trainers. It is strongly advised that

Ready     Back     Angle back

Over     Angle in     Straight in

*Casting signals.*

you seek the help of experienced trainers.

The verbal commands commonly used are "*Back*," meaning directly away from you, and "*Over*," meaning directly right or left. Your dog should already be whistle-trained to sit to one tweet, and to come toward you to a series of tweets. Hand signals are as follows:

• Arm extended straight up indicates "back"; extending the right arm tells the dog to twirl to the handler's right, and extending the left arm tells the dog to twirl to the handler's left, when turning away from the handler.

• Arm extended straight to the side indicates "over"; extending the right arm tells the dog to run to the right, and extending the left arm tells the dog to run to the left, in relation to the handler.

• Arm extended at an angle between vertical and horizontal is called an angle-back or angle-in cast, and to run at an angle, left or right, depending on which arm is used.

Because dogs work at long distances from the handler in field trials, handlers in trials usually wear white, or a color that will show up against the background, to increase the visibility of their signals. Leaning or stepping to the side while giving an arm signal also helps increase visibility.

### Baseball Diamond Handling

Professional trainers have many different ways of teaching dogs handling; the following is one possibility.

• Picture a baseball diamond configuration, with white cones at each base. You will give your directions from home plate. Eventually, birds or dummies will be planted at first, second, or third base positions, but start with a cone and birds (or dummies) only at a single (second) base.

• Let Max watch you toss several birds to second base. Heel him back to the pitcher's mound position, turn and say *"Dead bird,"* a phrase that will eventually tell him he's going to do a blind retrieve.

• Direct his attention to the second base cone, and when he is lined up correctly say *"That's it,"* again, a phrase Max will eventually learn means that he is lined up correctly. Then send him with the command *"Back"* and follow this with *"Fetch"*; the *fetch* will be omitted later once Max catches on.

• As Max returns to you with the bird, run backwards a few steps so he runs farther toward you. Then when he gives you the bird, send him back the same way for the next one, repeating the process and gradually getting farther and farther away with each send, until you are doing it from the home plate position.

• Once Max is running to second base reliably, let him watch you toss several more birds to second base. Have him sit facing you on the pitcher's mound, and send him from there, gradually increasing your distance from the pitcher's mound toward home plate, while Max remains on the mound facing you. This introduces him to the concept of facing you, and then twirling and running away from you on the back command.

• After this, place the birds at the cone out of Max's view and repeat

*Most Goldens enjoy water work most of all, but be careful not to send your enthusiastic, but exhausted, dog into deep water.*

**G O L D   N U G G E T**

### Dog Vision

Your dog's sensory world is different from yours. Dogs can see better at night because they have more receptors in their retinas called rods, which are more sensitive to dim light, and they have a reflective structure behind the retina called the tapetum lucidum, which is responsible for the glowing eyes your dog has at night when you shine a light in them. They see movement well, but because they have fewer cone receptors, which are needed for detail and color vision, they don't see details very well. They are also red-green color-blind (the technical term is deuteronopes), just like many red-green color-blind people. Dogs see blues and yellows just fine, but confuse shades of green, brown, and red with one another.

the process. For the first time Max will be retrieving something without ever having seen it fall, relying totally on his confidence in you.

• Now let Max watch you toss several birds on first base. Have him sit on the pitcher's mound facing you and command "*Over*," using a hand signal in which your arm is fully extended to the side toward which he should go. You should work your way back toward home plate, always sending him from the pitcher's mound.

• Do the same with third base, then present him with a mixture of bird placements. This whole process will take many sessions.

The baseball setup is also a good way to practice line drills. You want your dog to be able to rotate in *heel* position so that he is lined up with the base of your choice, and to run straight to retrieve the dummy at that base upon command. If he veers off toward another base, stop him with a voice command and call him back; if he continues, shorten the distance to the correct base. It's important that your dog take your direction rather than follow any preconceived idea he may have of the target's location.

### Directional Signal

One more all-important skill needs to be added before you can handle Max in the field. You must make him stop and look at you so he can see your next cast (directional signal). To do this you want him to stop, turn, and face you when told to do so, but getting him to stop when he's running full-blast toward the pile of dummies is asking a lot. Instead, call him toward you from second base; when he crosses the pitcher's mound, stop him with a single tweet, running toward him to stop him if necessary. When he stops, reward him by tossing the dummy or casting him to a base. Only after he is stopping reliably when coming toward you, should you try to stop him when running to retrieve the dummies. If he doesn't

*An enthusiastic water entry comes with practice and confidence.*

turn to face you—and many dogs will do so naturally—call him so that he must turn, and then tweet for him to stop again. When he is sitting and attending to you, cast him to one of the bases.

Now you have a dog that will go straight out, straight in (*come*), stop, go right, or go left on command. You can steer such a dog around obstacles and toward hidden birds. You can refine these skills over land and water. Start with very short blind retrieves and add more distance, cover, and complicated terrain. Place a cone by the bird so your directions will be accurate; it also helps the dog orient at first and gives him more confidence. As Max gets more proficient, use a less noticeable landmark. If he still finds the birds, it's time to go hunting!

If all of this sounds daunting, it can be. If it sounds like it will take a long time, it will. If it sounds like a lot of work, it is. If it sounds like a lot of fun, you bet!

### Field Terms

• Back: Command telling the dog to go directly away from the handler.
• Blind: A retrieving situation in which the dog does not see the fall; also, a shelter for shielding hunters.
• Blink: Failing to pick up a bird after finding it, often continuing to hunt.
• Break: Situation in which the dog leaves the handler to retrieve before being released or commanded to do so.

• Control: The degree to which the dog responds to direction, including obedience and manners on the line.

• Controlled break: Situation in which the dog begins to break but is quickly brought under control by the handler, using nonphysical means.

• Creeping: Situation in which the dog is unsteady, and may tentatively leave the handler, but is short of breaking; may also be caused by the dog adjusting its position to better see a mark.

• Delivery to hand: Situation in which the dog brings the bird to the handler and relinquishes it on command, without dropping, holding onto, or jumping after the bird.

• Diversion: A shot or thrown bird that could attract the dog's attention away from the intended bird.

• Double: Situation in which the dog must retrieve two birds, going back for one after retrieving the other.

• Gun (or Gunner): Person in the field who throws or shoots a dummy or bird.

• Handling: Directing the dog to a bird by means of whistle and hand signals.

• Hard mouth: Undesirable trait calling for a nonqualifying score in which the dog damages the bird, usually evidenced by crushed bones or extensive damage—rendering the bird unfit for human consumption—of the bird that could not have been caused by the fall or a zealous pickup.

*Puppies are into everything and tend to put everything into their mouths.*

• Honor: The dog's ability to watch another dog retrieve without interference.

• Line: The path a dog takes to the bird; it is expected to be straight, so that the dog "holds the line"; also, the starting point from which the dog is sent.

• Marking: The dog's ability to watch and remember where a bird has fallen, even if it is only the approximate location.

• Memory bird: In a multiple mark, the bird (or birds) that the dog retrieves after the first mark.

• Multiple mark: Situation in which more than one bird is thrown or shot before the dog is sent to retrieve them all.

• Nonslip retriever: A dog that stays at the hunter's side until sent.

• Over: Signal telling the dog to go in a direction at right angles to the handler.

• Perseverance: The extent to which a dog sticks with the task of searching for and returning a bird, and to repeatedly enter cold or rough water, rough cover, or other difficult circumstances, without quitting, slowing, switching birds, or otherwise giving up.

• Popping: Situation in which the dog stops on his own and looks back to the handler for direction and assistance, indicating lack of perseverance.

• Recast: Resending the dog after he starts toward a marked fall, but stops almost immediately after starting, usually indicating confusion about whether he was really sent.

• Refusal: Any disregard of a command, including refusal to cast, fetch, stop, change directions, or come.

• Response: The dog's adherence to the handler's directions and commands.

• Series: One or more hunting situations in which the dog must be called back by the judge to continue to compete in subsequent series.

• Steadiness: Ability to remain motionless on the line, with the exception of slight changes in position to see a fall.

• Style: The manner in which a dog works, indicated by its gaiety, obedience, alertness, speed, determination, aggressive searching, prompt pickup, and eagerness throughout.

• Switching: Giving up searching for, or dropping, one bird and picking up another instead.

• Trainability: Abilities acquired through training, especially steadiness, control, response, and delivery.

• Triple: Situation in which a dog must retrieve three birds, returning for the next after delivering the first, and then second, of them.

## Chapter Ten

# Going for Gold

You can share a perfect life with your Golden without ever entering any kind of competition, earning any kind of title, or winning any kind of ribbon. As any Golden owner knows, the best rewards of Golden ownership are the intangible ones. Many people, however, find that they so much enjoy activities with their Golden Retriever that they look for more challenges they can share. These can include conformation shows, obedience trials, tracking trials, agility trials, field trials, and hunting tests.

## Conformation Shows

Your Golden Retriever is no doubt pure gold in your eyes, and chances are, being a Golden Retriever, you're right. Your neighbors, friends, and veterinarian have probably commented on your dog's good looks. So it's only natural to want to show off your dog in a dog show.

As gorgeous as your Golden may be, unless your dog comes from a

*Any competition takes teamwork.*

line of dogs that have proven themselves in the show ring, chances are your dog may have some physical features that don't quite measure up to (or even approach) the standard of perfection (see page 15). You can still show your dog, as long as he or she is at least six months of age, is AKC registered, is neither spayed nor neutered, (if male) has two normally descended testicles, and has no disqualifying faults (see page 15). You may not win, but you'll learn a lot about the show world and be better prepared in case you want to show your next Golden (of course you will have another!). See page 29 for tips on finding a good Golden show prospect.

Show training involves striking a balance between obedience and exuberance. Picture your Golden in

GOLD ⭐ STAR

One of the breed's greats, Ch-AFCh Riverview's Chickasaw Thistle, UDT set the standard as a mistress of all trades.

the field, strutting around, proudly carrying a dummy or ball or looking attentively into the distance. You want your dog to show this same kind of animation and confidence in the ring. It helps if your Golden will "bait," that is, look attentively at a little tidbit or toy. The show dog must be able to stand posed even when the judge touches it from head to tail. The show pose is simply standing with the front legs parallel to each other and perpendicular to the ground, and the back legs also parallel to each other but set wider than the front legs, and with the hocks perpendicular to the ground. The head is held up and the tail is held horizontally, either naturally or by the handler.

It will take many outings before both you and your Golden will give a polished performance. You can practice at informal matches meanwhile, and if you're lucky, join a handling class. There are professional handlers who will show your dog for you and probably win more often than you would; however, there's

GOLD ★ STAR

Ch Signature's Sounds A Hopin' finished her Championship at the tender age of six months, an accomplishment all the more impressive when considering dogs cannot be shown until their six-month birthday!

## GOLD NUGGET

### To Pose Your Dog...

1. Walk the dog into a standing position and say "*Stand*."
2. Place your right hand under the dog's chin to control the head.
3. Shift the dog's weight toward you.
4. Place your left hand just under the dog's left elbow and move the leg so it falls straight down from the body and the foot points straight ahead.
5. Shift the dog's weight to the right and repeat for the left front leg.
6. Grasp the dog's right rear leg just above the "knee" (stifle), shift her weight off that side, and move the leg so it falls straight down from the hip, with the hock perpendicular to the ground and the feet pointing straight ahead.
7. Repeat for the other rear leg.
8. If the dog will bait, especially if she will hold her tail out by herself, then teach her to stay in place while you hold bait in front of her, occasionally rewarding her.
9. You can also stand beside the dog and hold the head up with your right hand and tail out with your left hand.
10. Make sure your dog isn't leaning backwards. If so, use bait to encourage her to lean forward, or gently pull her backward by the tail.

nothing like the thrill of winning when you're the one on the other end of the lead!

Once you feel that you're ready to try a real dog show, you should contact the AKC and ask for the free dog show regulation pamphlet, which will explain the requirements for each class. Your dog must be entered about three weeks before the show date, and you'll need to get a premium list and entry form from the appropriate show superintendent; their addresses are available from the AKC, most dog magazines, or the Internet. You may also wish to read additional books devoted entirely to dog show know-how.

**Classes:** You may enter any class for which your dog is eligible: Puppy, which may be divided into classes for 6–9 months and 9–12 months, 12–18 months, Novice, American Bred, Bred by Exhibitor, or Open, but you should enter only one class. The toughest competition is usually in the Bred by Exhibitor, Open, and of course, Best of Breed classes. The Best of Breed class is only for dogs that are already Champions. All the male (dog) classes are judged before all the female (bitch) classes. Each class winner within a sex competes in the Winners class for points toward the championship title. Each time a judge chooses your dog as the best dog of its sex that is not already a Champion, in other words, either Winners Dog or Winners Bitch, it wins up to 5 points, depending upon how many dogs it defeats. To become an AKC Cham-

GOLD NUGGET

**Gold Rulers**
Contact the AKC for complete rules for AKC events, or read them on-line at http://www.akc.org/insideAKC/resources/rulereg.cfm

pion (Ch), your Golden must win 15 points including two majors, defeating enough dogs to win 3 to 5 points at a time.

**Show leads:** Several different show leads are available. Most Golden handlers prefer a small choke collar and thin show lead. Experiment with different collar positions, which

*Preparing for competition should be enjoyable.*

133

GOLD ★ STAR

One of the most impressive Championship finishes was that of Ch Toby of Wollow Loch***, who finished his AKC Championship in three straight shows; at the third show he became the first American-bred Golden to win a Best in Show.

can influence the dog's head position and movement.

**Grooming:** Your dog will need to be perfectly show-groomed (see page 49) and you, too, should look professional in a sports suit or skirt. Be sure to wear flat rubber-soled shoes for running.

### The Ring

Get to the show early so you can get a feel for what's going on and get your dog acclimated, but don't get her overheated or tired. Locate your ring and watch the judge's pattern. Typically, the dogs in each class will enter in numerical order according to armbands (pick yours up from the ring steward about 15 minutes before Goldens are to be judged) and pose while the judge checks them in and looks them over. Then the entire class will trot around once or twice. After that, the judge will examine the first dog in line. The judge will then have that dog trot either directly away and back to him or her, or in a triangle. The procedure will be repeated until the last

dog has been examined. After that all the dogs are posed again, and the judge may move them or switch them around or make some tentative picks. If you're fortunate enough to win a ribbon, take it in stride; if not, take it in even better stride and congratulate the winner. One day that will be you.

### After the Show

Don't just fly back to your car or home after showing. Now that the pressure is off, you'll find many people who are eager to meet you and find out about your dog. Even after everyone has drifted off, take your dog on a tour of the dog supply stands and buy her a treat for being such a good sport. After all, your dog would probably have rather spent the day playing in the mud. Stay around and watch different handlers' grooming techniques and how they show their dogs. Watch the Sporting group and cheer on the Golden Best of Breed (BOB) winner. Stay for Best in Show (BIS) and cheer for the Sporting Group winner—hopefully the Golden. Don't make winning or losing the deciding factor as to whether or not you have fun at the show.

GOLD ★ STAR

The precocious Ch Touchstone's Oh Whad Ya Doo SDHF is the youngest Golden to win a BIS and the youngest with a SDHF designation.

Almost everyone who enters a dog show loses that day, because the only dog that remains undefeated at the end of the show is the Best in Show winner. This means that you need to be able to separate your own ego and self-esteem from your dog. You can't let your dog's ability to win in the ring cloud your perception of her true worth in her primary role: that of friend and companion. Because Goldens are so much a true family member, it can hurt to have your beloved dog placed last in her class. Just be sure that your dog doesn't catch on, and always treat your dog like a Best in Show winner whether she gets a blue ribbon or no ribbon at all. As long as you do that, you will always be a winner at the end of the show.

*To compete is the glory; to win is the honor.*

## Obedience Trials

Part of the pleasure of living with Goldens is their amenability to training, and their ability to pick up new ideas quickly. The exuberant Golden especially profits from having her intellectual energy directed into acceptable behaviors. Training a Golden Retriever is so rewarding that many people choose to go beyond basic training and teach more advanced obedience. They also find that demonstrating their Golden's abilities at obedience trials is a great way to challenge themselves to polish their performances and learn new skills.

In an obedience trial, each dog's performance of a set group of exer-

cises is evaluated against a standard of perfection. Several organizations, including the AKC and United Kennel Club (UKC), sponsor obedience trials, with progressively more difficult levels. The AKC is the most popular venue in the United States, so it will be the one described here. UKC exercises are similar, but slightly more difficult.

GOLD ★ STAR

One of the breed's obedience greats was OTCh Topbrass Ric O Shay Barty, OHF, OS, who amassed 3,600 OTCh points in his 11-year career. He was the top obedience dog of all breeds for two years. One of his most memorable wins was a perfect 200 score in Open at 13 years of age, when he retired with his 150th High in Trial.

GOLD ★ STAR

American Canadian Ch Des Lacs Lassie CD OD was the first Golden bitch to win Best in Show; she also won the GRCA National specialty twice and at one time held the record for champion off-spring.

**Novice:** Novice is the lowest level of AKC competition. To earn the Companion Dog (CD) title a dog must qualify at three trials. Each qualifying score is called a "leg" and requires passing each individual exercise and earning a total score of at least 170 points out of a possible 200 points.

The Novice exercises are:
• Heel on lead, sitting automatically each time you stop, negotiating right, left, and about turns without guidance from you, and changing to a faster and slower pace.
• Heel in a figure 8 around two people, still on lead.
• Stand still off lead 6 feet (1.8 m) away from you and allow a judge to touch your dog.
• Do the same heeling exercises as before except off lead.
• Come to you when called from 20 feet (6.1 m) away, and then return to *heel* position on command.
• Stay in a sitting position with a group of other dogs, while you are 20 feet (6.1 m) away, for one minute.
• Stay in a *down* position with the same group while you are 20 feet (6.1 m) away, for three minutes.

**Open:** Open is the intermediate level of AKC competition. To be awarded the Companion Dog Excellent (CDX) title, a dog must earn three legs performing these Open exercises:
• Heel off lead, including a figure 8.
• Come when called from 20 feet (6.1 m) away, but dropping to a *down* position when told to do so partway to you, then completing the recall when called again.
• Retrieve a thrown dumbbell when told to do so.
• Retrieve a thrown dumbbell, leaving, and returning over a high jump.
• Jump over a broad jump when told to do so.
• Stay in a sitting position with a group of dogs, when you are out of sight, for three minutes.
• Stay in a *down* position with a group of dogs, when you are out of sight, for five minutes.

**Utility:** Utility is the highest level of AKC competition. To earn the Utility Dog (UD) title, a dog must

GOLD ★ STAR

The all-time top-winning AKC show Golden is Ch Asterling's Wild Blue Yonder, winner of 51 Best in Show awards and 146 group firsts; the all-time top-winning female is Ch Brandymist's QB Gal.

G O L D ⭐ S T A R

Ch Rush Hill's Hagen Daaz has won more Golden specialty shows than any other Golden in history; Ch Sassafras Batteries Not Included has won the National Specialty a phenomenal four times.

earn three legs performing these Utility exercises:

• *Heel, stay, sit, down,* and *come* in response to hand signals.

• Retrieve a leather article scented by the handler from among five other unscented articles.

• Retrieve a metal article scented by the handler from among five other unscented articles.

• Retrieve a glove designated by the handler from among three gloves placed in different locations.

• Stop and stand on command while heeling and allow the judge to physically examine it with the handler standing 10 feet (3 m) away.

• Trot away from the handler for about 40 feet (12 m) until told to stop, at which point the dog should turn and sit, until directed to jump one of two jumps—a solid or bar jump—and return to the handler.

• Repeat the previous exercise, but jumping the opposite jump as before.

Owners of most breeds would give themselves a hearty congratulations for what often amounts to years of work in achieving the UD

title. Many owners of UD Goldens are just getting started, though. The Utility Dog Excellent (UDX) is awarded to a dog, which must already have its UD, to earn 10 legs in both Open (CDX) and Utility classes at the same trials.

**OTCh:** The supreme AKC obedience title is the Obedience Trial Champion (OTCh). Unlike other obedience titles that require only performance to a standard proficiency, points toward the OTCh require performance of such precision that it is scored ahead of other passing dogs. A dog that places first or second in either Open or Utility classes earns a certain amount of points depending on how many dogs were in competition. It takes 100 points, plus three first placements, to earn the OTCh; understandably, very few dogs in any breed can claim such a prestigious title. That is, except for Goldens. In Goldens, the OTCh is still an extremely coveted and difficult goal, but an obtainable one.

**HIT:** The top award at an obedience trial is High in Trial (HIT), given to the top scoring dog from any regular class. Generations of attention to temperament and intelligence

G O L D ⭐ S T A R

The first Golden to earn a UD was Goldwood Toby UD; the first to earn a UDT (UD and TD) was his son, Featherquest Trigger UDT.

have placed the Golden among the top HIT winners of all breeds.

If you enter competition with your Golden, remember this as your Golden Rule: Companion Dog means just that; being upset at your dog because she made a mistake defeats the purpose of obedience as a way of promoting a harmonious partnership between trainer and dog. Failing a trial, in the scope of life, is an insignificant event. Never let a ribbon or a few points become more important than a trusting relationship with your companion. Be sure you fulfill your responsibility as a Companion Human before demanding that your Golden be a Companion Dog. Besides, your dog will forgive you for the times *you* mess up!

## Tracking Trials

One of the more mysterious, awe-inspiring, useful, and enjoyable canine abilities for which tests and titles are available is tracking; yet it is a curious fact that tracking is one of the least popular of AKC competitions. Part of this probably lies in the

---

G O L D ★ S T A R

The first OTCh of any breed was the Golden OTCh Moreland's Golden Tonka; she completed the requirements in a dazzling 23 days. During her amazing career, Tonka won eight perfect scores and was 176 times High in Trial. In fact, the first three dogs of all breeds to earn an OTCh were Goldens.

---

fact that it does require a lot of time training alone, but on the other hand, that's part of its appeal. What better excuse to share a quiet misty morning in the field with your dog?

The way to start training depends upon what motivates your dog. For chowhounds, you can begin by walking a simple path and dropping little treats along it. The dog will soon learn that she can find treats simply by following your trail. As training progresses, drop the treats farther and farther apart, until eventually only the motherlode of treats is left at the end of the trail.

If your dog is motivated more by the desire to be with you, you can have a helper hold her while you hide a very short distance away. Then the helper allows the dog to find you. Gradually increase the distance and make sure the dog is using her nose to locate you.

Of course, the actual tracking tests will require considerably more training than this, but once you have

---

G O L D ★ S T A R

Few dogs of any breed have won a Best in Show and a High in Trial; even fewer have done it at the same show, as did Am Can Ch Beckwith's Malagold Flash, Am Can UDT, WC.

taught your dog to follow her nose, you're on the right track.

The AKC offers several tracking titles:

**The AKC Tracking Dog (TD)** title is earned by following a 440- to 500-yard (402 to 457 m) track with three to five turns laid by a person from 30 minutes to 2 hours before.

**The Tracking Dog Excellent (TDX)** title is earned by following an "older" (three to five hours) and longer (800- to 1,000-yard [732 to 914 m]) track with five to seven turns, with some more challenging circumstances. One of these circumstances is the existence of cross tracks laid by another tracklayer about an hour and a half after the first track was laid. In addition, the actual track may cross various types of terrain and obstacles, including plowed land, woods, streams, bridges, and lightly traveled roads.

**The Variable Surface Tracking (VST)** title is earned by following a three- to five-hour track, 600 to 800 yards (549 to 732 m) long, over a variety of surfaces such as might be normally encountered when tracking in the real world. At least three different surface areas are included, of which at least one must include vegetation, and at least two must be devoid of vegetation, for example, sand or concrete. Tracks may even go through buildings, and may be crossed by animal, pedestrian, or vehicular traffic.

The title of Champion Tracker (CT) is awarded to a dog that earns all three tracking titles.

# Agility Trials

The fastest-growing canine sport is that of agility. Agility is an obstacle course for dogs run against the clock, combining jumping, balancing, climbing, weaving, running through tunnels, and lots of fun!

The AKC, United States Dog Agility Association (USDAA), and United Kennel Club (UKC) sponsor trials and award titles. In fact, the USDAA is the original sponsor of agility trials in the United States and still one of the most popular organizations. We will describe the AKC program here, although all the programs are similar in concept.

The obstacles are arranged in various configurations that vary from trial to trial. Handlers can give unlimited commands, but cannot touch the obstacles or dog or use food, toys, whistles, or any training or guiding devices in the ring. Points are lost for refusing an obstacle, knocking down a jump, missing a contact zone, taking obstacles out

*G O L D    N U G G E T*

**Fun on the Web**

The Dog Agility Page
http://www.dogpatch.org/agility/

The Tracking Page
http://personal.cfw.com/~dtratnac/

The Dog Obedience and Training Page
http://www.dogpatch.org/obed/

GOLD ★ STAR

The first Champion Tracker was CT-Can Ch Westbury Golden Pine Escapade CDX TDX, who earned the title in 1997.

of sequence, and exceeding the allotted time limit. To get a qualifying score, a dog must earn 85 out of a possible 100 points with no non-qualifying deductions.

Classes are divided by height, with most Goldens competing in the two highest height divisions—18 to 22 inches (46 to 56 cm), and 22 inches and over, at the withers. These dogs jump heights of 20 and 24 inches (51 and 61 cm), respectively.

The obstacles and their requirements are:

• The A-Frame requires the dog to climb over two 8- or 9-feet-long (2.4 or 2.7-m) boards, each 3 to 4 feet (.91 to 1.2 m) wide, positioned so they form an A-frame with the peak about 5 to 5½ feet (1.5 to 1.7 m) off the ground.

• The Dog Walk requires the dog to climb a sloping panel and walk across a suspended section and down another sloping panel. Each panel is 1 foot (30 cm) wide and either 8 or 12 feet (2.4 or 3.6 m) long, and the horizontal bridge section is 3 or 4 feet (.91 to 1.2 m) high.

• The Seesaw requires the dog to traverse the entire length of a 1-foot-wide by 12-feet-long (.30 by 3 m) sloping panel supported near its

*A Golden sails through an agility course.*

center by a fulcrum base, so that when the dog passes the center the plank teeters to rest on its other end.
• The Pause Table requires the dog to stop and either sit or lie down for five seconds on top of a table approximately 3 feet (.91 m) square, and either 16 or 24 inches (41 or 61 cm) high, depending on the height category.
• The Open Tunnel requires the dog to run through a flexible tube, about 2 feet (61 cm) in diameter and 10 to 20 feet (3 to 6 m) long, and curved so that the dog cannot see the exit from the entrance.
• The Closed Tunnel requires the dog to run through a lightweight fabric chute about 12 to 15 feet (3.6 to 4.6 m) long, with a rigid entrance of about 2 feet (61 cm) in diameter.
• The Weave Poles require the dog to weave from left to right through an entire series of 6 to 12, each spaced 20 to 24 inches (51 to 61 cm) apart.
• The Single Bar Jumps require the dog to jump over a high jump consisting of a narrow bar without knocking it off. Other single jumps are also permitted.
• The Panel Jump requires the dog to jump over a high jump consisting of a solid-appearing wall without displacing the top panel.
• The Double Bar Jump (or Double Oxer) requires the dog to jump two parallel bars positioned at the jump heights specified for the Single Bar Jump, and situated a distance of one-half the jump height from each other.

## GOLD NUGGET

### How Do Dogs Trail?
Wherever we go, we raise a commotion by crushing plants and stirring up dirt. We also leave behind traces of sweat, skin, exhaled air, and perfumes. Dogs can detect minute amounts of these odors and follow them.

• The Triple Bar Jump requires the dog to jump a series of three ascending bars, in which the horizontal distance between adjacent bars is one-half the jump height, and the vertical distance is one-quarter the jump height.
• The Tire Jump (or Circle Jump) requires the dog to jump through a circular object, approximately 2 feet (61 cm) in diameter, resembling a tire suspended from a rectangular frame, with the bottom of opening at the same height as the Single Bar Jump.
• The Window Jump requires the dog to jump through a 2-foot (61-cm) square (or diameter) window opening with the bottom of the opening at the same height as the Single Bar Jump.
• The Broad Jump requires the dog to perform a single jump over a spaced series of either four 8-inch (20-cm)- or five 6-inch (15-cm)-wide sections.

Because safety is of utmost importance, all official jumps have easily displaceable bars in case the dog fails to clear them. All climbing

G O L D ★ S T A R

A master of versatility, Ch Timberee's Olympic Gasparilla UD, WC, JH AX, VCX, ODHF was the first champion to also earn his AX.

obstacles have contact zones painted near the bottom that the dog must touch rather than jumping off the top. All contact equipment surfaces are roughened for good traction in both dry and wet weather.

AKC agility is divided into two types: the standard agility classes that include all the obstacles, and Jumpers With Weaves (JWW) agility classes. The latter is a faster-paced version of agility that emphasizes jumping and speed without the careful control needed for the pause table and contact points in the standard obedience class. Titles for the standard agility classes are NA for Novice, OA for Open, and AX for Excellent, and MX for Master. JWW titles are the same with a J added to the end: NAJ, OAJ, AXJ, and MXJ.

For standard agility:

**1.** The Novice class uses 12 to 13 obstacles, including the A-Frame, Pause Table, Dog Walk, Open Tunnel, Seesaw, Closed Tunnel, Broad Jump, Panel Jump, Double Bar Jump, either the Tire Jump or Window Jump, and two or three additional obstacles (excluding the One Bar and Triple Bar Jumps).

**2.** The Open class uses 15 to 17 obstacles, including the ten manda-tory obstacles from the Novice class plus Weave Poles and four to six additional obstacles. The latter may include one Triple Bar Jump but cannot include the One Bar Jump.

**3.** The Excellent class uses 18 to 20 obstacles, including all the Open Class obstacles, except that the Broad Jump is optional, plus the Triple Bar Jump, One Bar Jump, and additional jumps or tunnel to meet the required number of obstacles.

For Jumpers With Weaves classes:

**1.** The Novice JWW class uses 13 to 15 obstacles, including one Double Bar Jump, one series of six Weave Poles, and the remainder Single Bar Jumps.

**2.** The Open JWW class uses 16 to 18 obstacles, including one Double Bar Jump, one Triple Bar Jump, one series of six to twelve Weave Poles, and the remainder Single Bar Jumps and One Bar Jumps.

**3.** The Excellent JWW uses 18 to 20 obstacles, one Double Bar Jump,

G O L D ★ S T A R

The top agility Golden of all time is ADCh FlashPaws Hollywood Hotshot UDX, MX, MXJ, BDA-CD, who was the first Golden to win the MXJ title, and second, after her dam, to earn the MX. Holly twice represented the United States at the Agility World Championships as part of the U.S. Agility Team, and is also nearing her OTCh.

one Triple Bar Jump, one series of ten to twelve Weave Poles, and the remainder Single Bar Jumps and One Bar Jumps.

In addition, the courses may optionally include the Open Tunnel, Closed Tunnel, Broad Jump, Panel Jump, Tire Jump, and Window Jump.

It gets tougher, though. One of the major challenges of an agility course is the complex course the dog must take from obstacle to obstacle. This course includes tougher challenges at higher levels of competition. For example, the obstacles may have to be approached from sharp angles (up to 90 degrees in Novice, 135 degrees in Open, and 180 degrees in Excellent). Courses may also include Call-Offs, in which the dog must not jump an obstacle in its path, Options and Traps, in which the dog must jump only one of two obstacles at a decision point, Side-Switches, in which the course makes an S-curve, requiring the handler to switch from one side of the dog to the other, and Lead-Out Advantages, in which handlers who can run ahead of their dogs while the dog remains steady at the start line or pause table are at an advantage.

Many obedience clubs are now sponsoring agility training, but you can start some of the fundamentals at home. Entice your dog to walk through a tunnel made of sheets draped over chairs; guide her with treats to weave in and out of a series of poles made from several plumber's helpers placed in line; make her comfortable walking on a

*G O L D   N U G G E T*

**Other Agility Organizations**

United States Dog Agility
 Association (USDAA)
P.O. Box 850995
Richardson, Texas 75085-0955
Tel: (972) 231-9700
E-mail: info@usdaa.com
http://www.usda.com

Agility Association of Canada
 (AAC)
957 Seymour Boulevard
North Vancouver,
 British Columbia V7J 2J7
Tel: (604) 230-4225
E-mail: coronet@portal.ca
http://www.aac.ca/

North American Dog Agility
 Council (NADAC)
HCR 2, Box 277
St. Maries, Idaho 83861
Tel: (208) 689-3803
E-mail: nelsonk9@iea.com

Canine Performance Events
 (CPE)
P.O. Box 445
Walled Lake, MI 48390
E-mail: cpe-agility@juno.com

wide raised board; teach her to jump through a tire and over a hurdle. Teach your dog some basic obedience commands (*sit, down, come, and stay*), and make sure she is

*Training for competition starts young with socialization and an introduction to the game. Here a future agility star gets acquainted with the teeter-totter.*

comfortable and under control around other dogs.

You need to condition your Golden like any athlete to compete in agility. You also need to have a health check beforehand, making sure your dog is not dysplastic, arthritic, or visually impaired. High jumping and vigorous weaving can impose stresses on immature bones, so these should be left until adulthood.

## Field Trials

Whether you train your dog yourself, or have someone else do it, the day will come when your dog has the basic skills to be a top-notch hunting partner and a successful hunt test prospect. The really fun part will be honing them to perfection. Although the ultimate reward for a well-trained retriever is a reliable hunting companion, it's also fun to test your dog against some stan-

GOLD ★ STAR

Only two Goldens have earned championships in both field and obedience competition: Canadian FTCh/OTCh Windbreaker Bulrush Buddy and Canadian FTCh/OTCh Kipp's Cotton Jenny.

dards of performance or against other retrievers. Field events also offer a challenging outlet when hunting season is over. There are plenty of venues from which to choose, and lots of titles to be won. Some are offered by different organizations, but the major distinction is between a test and a trial. In a test, dogs are judged against a standard set of performance criteria rather than each other. In a trial, dogs are judged against the performance of other dogs. Trials are unquestionably the more difficult venue.

Field trials test a dog's natural instincts and training over both land and water. Marking tests and blind retrieves are deliberately difficult, requiring the dog to take a route to the fall over obstacles and terrain that test a dog's memory and perseverance in reaching the fall, which may be over 250 yards (229 m). Land obstacles include uneven terrain, gullies, brush, trees, logs, and hay bales, among others. Water obstacles include islands, sandbars, irregular shorelines, points of land, and vegetation, among others. A field trial simulates real hunting in the sense that comparable situations are sometimes encountered during exceptionally difficult circumstances in the field. It differs from real hunting in the sense that such challenging situations don't normally appear on every fall, nor even every hunt. Not only must a dog competing in field trials overcome extraordinarily demanding challenges, but to win points, a dog must overcome these

**G O L D   N U G G E T**

## What Those *'s Mean

Often Goldens have asterisks as part of their titles, which designate the following:

   * WC

  ** Any Placement or a Judge's Award of Merit (JAM) in Derby, or a third or fourth placement of a JAM in a Qualifying stake in an AKC trial.

*** "Qualified All-Age Dog," which means a first or second placement in a Qualifying stake, or any placement of a JAM in Open All-Age Stake at an AKC trial.

*Sometimes the hardest part is waiting.*

G O L D ★ S T A R

The first Golden Retriever Field Champion was FC Rip, born in 1935 and the last pick of his litter. By 18 months of age, he had finished his title; he later was the top-winning retriever of any breed for 1939 and 1940. Unfortunately, Rip died in his prime as a five-year-old, but he left an inspirational image for many Golden trainers that followed.

challenges in a manner better than the many other talented retrievers, representing all retrieving breeds, not just Goldens, in competition. The high caliber of competition necessitates this gauntlet of tests in order to separate the dogs that are truly great from those that are merely fabulous.

Four stakes are offered at AKC sponsored field trials:

**1.** *The Derby Stake* is for dogs under two years of age. The emphasis is on marking ability and style, with retrieves usually limited to single and double marks, usually with the bird throwers (called guns or gunners) remaining visible. Two series are usually done on land, and two on water. Dogs win from 1 to 5 Derby points for first through fourth placements. Dogs that accumulate at least 10 Derby points appear on the "Derby List," and the dog earning the most Derby points during the year is declared the High-Point Derby Dog.

**2.** *The Qualifying Stake* is for dogs that have not won two Qualifying Stakes, nor received a Judge's Award of Merit in the Open All-Age Stake, and have not received a placement in the Amateur All-Age Stake. Both marking tests and blind retrieves are included, although the blind retrieves aren't usually as complicated as in higher-level stakes. The marking tests are usually triple retrieves with all guns visible, although occasionally, gunners may hide after throwing their bird. A dog that places first or second in a Qualifying Stake, or that receives a Judge's Award of Merit or better in a major stake, is said to be Qualified All-Age, and Goldens that earn this are designated by the GRCA with three asterisks (***) after their name. Dogs so designated may compete in Limited All-Age Stakes, which are offered at some large trials.

**3.** *The Open All-Age Stake* is open to all AKC-registered retrievers, but are best not entered except by dogs with well-honed skills. Dogs must be steady at all times. Tests are challenging, commonly including triple or quadruple marks (with and without retired guns), and single, double, or triple blind retrieves. The trial usually begins with the land tests, and only those performing well are called back to try the water tests. Championship points are awarded toward the Field Champion (FC) title, with first place worth 5 points, down to fourth place, which is worth one-half point. The FC title requires 10 points, with one first placement earned in all-breed competition. The dog amassing the most Open All-Age Stake points during the calendar year is awarded the prestigious High-Point Open Dog Award.

**4.** *The Amateur All-Age Stake* differs from the Open All-Age Stake only in that the handlers must be amateurs. An amateur is defined as someone who has not earned any fees from training or handling a dog for hunting or field trial competition during the preceding year. Points earned from placements in this stake count toward the Amateur Field Champion (AFC) title. The AFC title requires 15 points, with one first placement (or 10 points earned in Open or Limited All-Age stakes, if handled by an amateur). The dog amassing the most Amateur All-Age Stake points during the calendar year is awarded the prestigious High-Point Amateur Dog Award.

The zenith of all AKC field titles are the National Field Champion (NFC) and National Amateur Field Champion (NAFC), awarded to the winners of the annual National Open Retriever Championship Stake, held each November, and the National Amateur Retriever Championship Stake, held each June. To be eligible to compete in either, a dog must have earned at least 7 points, including a win placement, in the appropriate (Open or Amateur) All-Age Stake. The previous year's NFC and NAFC are also eligible, and if the current NFC is amateur handled, that dog is also eligible to compete in the NAFC.

# Hunting Tests

Dogs that compete in field trials represent retrieving skills at their zenith, but most people don't have the time or ability, let alone dog, to make it to that level. In hunting tests, dogs are evaluated against a standard, rather than in competition with other dogs. After all, as long as your dog performs her duties satisfactorily, does it really matter if another dog does it a little better? Rather than test how well a dog performs under situations so challenging they are the exception, rather than the rule, in a day's hunting, hunting tests evaluate how well a dog performs when faced with somewhat more typical retrieves and conditions found in a day's hunt. Tests are offered by several different organizations, and even though the

GOLD ★ STAR

A double-header refers to the rare and prestigious occasion in which the same dog wins both the Open and Amateur Stakes at the same trial. The first Golden to win a Double Header was FC-AFC Misty's Sungold Lad, CDX, who accomplished the feat twice in 1969. Three Goldens have also won a double-header at the GRCA National Specialty: FC-AFC Tigathoes Magic Marker, Splashdown Texas Two Stepper, and FC-AFC Valhaven Smokin Vindaloo.

GOLD ★ STAR

The all-time high-point field Golden, NAFC-FC Topbrass Cotton, is the only Golden to win the National Amateur Field Trial.

tests differ slightly, they share the basic premise of providing a realistic means by which a good hunting companion can be recognized.

## AKC Tests

The AKC offers several popular hunt tests for retrievers. Judges score each dog on a scale of 1 to 10 for marking, style, perseverance, and trainability, the latter demonstrated by steadiness, response, control, and delivery. In order to pass, a dog must receive an overall average score of at least 7, with an average of at least 5 in each category and no scores of zero.

**1.** *The Junior Hunter Test* consists of four single marks of less than 100 yards (91 m), with two on land and two on water. Dogs should be steady but may be gently restrained. They must deliver to hand. A dog that qualifies at four Junior Hunter tests earns the Junior Hunter (JH) title.

**2.** *The Senior Hunter Test* consists of two blind retrieves (one on land, one on water), two double marks (one on land, one on water), a walk-up, a diversion shot and/or mark, and an honor. In a walk-up, the dog walks off lead at the handler's side, sits when the bird is thrown, and remains sitting while birds are being shot. In an honor, the dog is required to stay in place while in the vicinity of another working dog. The terrain is usually more challenging than that found in a Junior Hunter test. Dogs must be steady and cannot be restrained on the line. A dog that qualifies at five Senior Hunter (or four Senior Hunter if it already has the JH title) tests earns the title of Senior Hunter (SH).

**3.** *The Master Hunter Test* consists of land and water blinds, multiple (double and triple) marks on land and water (and combined multiples on land and water), a walk-up, diversion shots and/or marks, and an honor. The terrain is extremely challenging. Shot fliers are used in several of the marks. A dog that qualifies at six Master Hunter tests, or five Master Hunter tests if the dog is already a Senior Hunter, earns the title of Master Hunter (MH). The annual Master National is open to dogs that have earned the MH title and passed a minimum number of Master tests during the previous year. It is a grueling week-long series of tests that requires consistent high-caliber performances in order to pass.

GOLD ★ STAR

The first National Retriever Trial was held in 1941; the winner was a Golden Retriever named NFC/FC King Midas of Woodend.

## GRCA Tests

The Golden Retriever Club of America offers noncompetitive tests in which Goldens with moderate training can demonstrate their natural abilities. Tests are conducted on both land and water.

**1.** *The Working Certificate (WC) Test* is the simpler of the two, and is designed to demonstrate the dog's natural ability rather than its degree of training. The WC test is conducted and judged in a manner similar to the AKC Derby trials, with the exceptions that dogs are not expected to be steady, decoys are not used, delivery to hand is not required, and no maximum age limit is in place. Because the WC test is a marking test, the handler cannot direct the dog to the birds. The handler may, however, gently guide (not force) the dog to the line and between birds on the land double, and hold the dog back from breaking. The WC consists of:

• Land Double, in which the dog must retrieve two upland birds from moderate cover on land, without switching birds or refusing. The birds are located at least 90 degrees apart and about 40 to 50 yards (36 to 46 m) from the line.

• Back-to-Back Water Singles, in which the dog must retrieve two ducks from light cover in water on consecutive sends without refusing. The ducks are about 25 to 30 yards (23 to 27 m) from the line.

*The Working Certificate Excellent (WCX) Test* is a more advanced version, conducted and judged in a

**GOLD NUGGET**

### GRCA Awards

The GRCA offers the SDHF (Show Dog Hall of Fame), ODHF (Obedience Dog Hall of Fame), and FDHF (Field Dog Hall of Fame) designations to high achievers in their respective areas of competition, and the VC (Versatility Certificate) and VCX (Versatility Excellent Certificate) to dogs that have proved they can excel in several areas of competition. For the SDHF, a dog must amass 25 points by winning various awards—a Best in Show is worth 10 points, a Sporting Group First or National Specialty Best of Breed is worth 5 points, and other group placements and specialty show wins are worth slightly fewer points. For the ODHF, a dog must hold the UD title and win five High in Trials, three from an advanced class. For the FDHF, a dog must amass 25 points at licensed field trials, or win the National Field Trial.

manner similar to AKC Qualifying trials. The dog is off lead and collarless throughout the test and is not to be touched by the handler. The dog must remain steady at the line until the judge gives the signal to send. Birds must be delivered to hand and relinquished readily. The WCX consists of:

• Land Triple, in which the dog must retrieve three upland game birds, the first two dead, the last bird a flier, in moderate cover on land. The birds shall fall at least 60 degrees apart, separated by between 60 and 100 yards (55 to 91 m) apart. They shall fall at a 45-degree angle back from the guns.

• Water Double, in which the dog must retrieve two ducks from the water, one of which is in moderate cover not visible from the line, ideally about 45 yards (41 m) from the line. The second bird should fall about 60 yards (55 m) from the line in open swimming water. Two to four decoys will be present, but not in a direct line with either fall.

## North American Hunting Retriever Association Tests

The North American Hunting Retriever Association (NAHRA) sponsors noncompetitive field tests by which retrievers at various stages of training can be evaluated. Although most noncompetitive titles are placed after a dog's name, NAHRA titles are placed before the dog's name.

**1.** *Beginner tests* are designed as informal opportunities for inexperienced dogs. No formal rules or titles are associated with these tests, with the emphasis on familiarization and fun for both dog and handler. Dogs can be held on the line, and the retrieves are short, single retrieves of birds, or occasionally, bumpers, which need not be delivered to hand.

**2.** *Started tests* are the easiest of the true NAHRA tests. As in the beginner test, dogs can be held on the line, and delivery to hand is not required. The test consists of five single mark retrieves, two each on land—not to exceed 75 yards (68.5 m)—and two each on water—not to exceed 50 yards (46 m)—with the fifth on either land or water. A dog passing with an average score of at least 80 percent earns 2.5 points toward the 10 points needed for the Started Retriever (SR) title.

**3.** *Intermediate tests* add tougher requirements. The dog must be steady at the line and must deliver to hand. The test consists of an upland hunting test without a flushed bird, during which the dog should actively quarter a field and demonstrate control, a blind retrieve on water, not to exceed 50 yards (46 m), a double-marked retrieve on land, not to exceed 100 yards (91 m), a double-marked retrieve on water, not to exceed 75 yards (46 to 64 m), and a trailing test, in which the dog must trail a dragged dead bird for about 50 to 70 yards (46 to 64 m), including a turn. A dog passing with an average score of at least 80 percent earns 5 points toward the 20 points needed for the Working Retriever (WR) title.

G O L D ★ S T A R

One of the breed's busiest dogs has to be MHR Phoebe's Prize Piponia CDX MH OA WCX, who earned an amazing 12 titles within a dizzying 22 months.

*Several advanced exercises require your Golden to jump.*

**4.** *Senior tests* are a tough test of a dog's ability. They add a flushed bird test in which the dog must be steady to both shot and fall. The test consists of an upland hunting test with a flushed bird, a blind retrieve on land, not to exceed 100 yards (91 m), a blind retrieve on water, not to exceed 100 yards (91 m), a triple-marked retrieve on land, not to exceed 100 yards (91 m), a triple-marked retrieve on water, not to exceed 100 yards (91 m), and a trailing test. To complicate matters, one of the blind retrieves must be incorporated into one of the triple-marked retrieves. A dog passing with an aver-age score of at least 80 percent earns 20 points toward the Master Hunting Retriever (MHR) or the Grand Master Hunting Retriever (GMHR) title. The MHR requires 100 points, except that a dog that already has a Working Retriever (WR) title only needs 80 points. The GMHR requires 300 points.

The NAHRA offers a couple of special awards. One is the Brass Band award, given to dogs that qualify in either four Started or four Intermediate tests within a calendar year. These dogs are also invited to compete in one of eight Started/Intermediate Regional Invitational

Field Tests held the next year. At a higher level, a dog that qualifies in five Senior tests between May 1 and April 30, or that earns its MHR title by April 30 of the preceding year, is invited to compete in the prestigious Richard A. Wolters (RAW)/NAHRA Invitational Field Test.

## Hunting Retriever Club Tests

The Hunting Retriever Club (HRC) is affiliated with the UKC, but dogs need not be UKC-registered to compete at their first trials. It began in the 1980s, and grew out of dissatisfaction with what were thought to be unrealistically tough requirements encountered in the field trials of that time. In keeping with the idea that these are to be as close to real hunting scenarios as possible, the handler is the one to actually shoot the gun, which is loaded with blanks.

**1.** *The Started Test* consists of four single marks (two on land, two on water), with distances usually under 75 yards (68.5 m) on land and 50 yards (46 m) on water. Dogs can be gently restrained at the line. A qualifying dog earns 5 points, with a maximum of 10 points from Started trials counting toward titles.

**2.** *The Seasoned Hunting Test* consists of blind land and water retrieves, usually under 50 yards (46 m), and double land, under 100 yards (91 m), and water, under 75 yards (68.5 m). Dogs must be steady and deliver to hand. A qualifying dog earns 10 points, with a maximum of 40 points from Seasoned trials counting toward titles. The Hunter Retriever

(HR) title requires 40 points earned from Seasoned tests, or a combination of 30 points in Seasoned tests and 10 points in Started Tests.

**3.** *The Finished Hunting Test* consists of blind land and water retrieves, multiple (usually triple) land and water marks, an honor, and sometimes an upland test. A qualifying dog earns 15 points. The Hunting Retriever Champion (HRCH) title requires 100 points, with a maximum of 40 points coming from Started or Seasoned tests.

**4.** *The Upland Hunting Retriever Test* (UH) includes flushed birds, a walk-up (in which the dog is walking beside the handler and must remain steady when a bird is thrown), and an honor. Each pass is worth 10 points; the Upland Hunter (UH) title requires 40 points.

The highest title is the Grand Hunting Retriever Champion (GR. HRCH), awarded to dogs that earn 220 points at the Finished level and qualify at two Grand hunting tests, open only to dogs that have earned an additional 100 points beyond the HRCH.

# At a Test or Trial

You should attend a test or trial as a spectator before entering one. Find out if unentered dogs can attend; exposing your dog to the trial activities will be good acclimatization. Under no circumstances can you bring a female in season on the trial grounds, nor should you bring a dog that is unruly or loud. Leave your dog crated at first until you find out where unentered dogs can be. Keep your dog on a leash; it would be terrible if it ruined a competing dog's run. It is good manners to keep your voice, and your dog's voice, down when a dog is being run. By the same token, because field trial handlers usually wear all white to increase their visibility when handling a dog at a distance, you should not wear white; you could distract a dog that was looking for signals from its handler and instead focused on you in your white shirt.

Take this opportunity to watch what the handlers do:
• Good handlers check in with the Marshall when they arrive and are ready for their turn.
• Good handlers don't manhandle their dogs on the line.
• Good handlers will watch their dog, making sure their dog is watching the guns before indicating they are ready.
• Good handlers don't send their dogs until told to do so by the judge, and even then wait until their dog is looking toward the area where the bird fell.
• Good handlers allow their dog to creep a bit if they know that by signaling the dog to stay, it will have no effect and only alert the judges to the fact the dog is breaking.
• Good handlers reach for the bird when the dog is supposed to deliver to hand but appears it may instead be in the process of dropping it. They don't hesitate to handle (where the rules allow) as soon as it appears the dog needs help.
• Good handlers understand what they did wrong, and ask the advice of other handlers.
• Good handlers know the rules for the particular organization and test they are running.
• Most of all, good handlers have fun, enjoy their dog, their fellow entrants, and a great time in the field. They understand that competing is the fun part, winning is the dream, and if they don't make it there's always another day.

Don't expect to qualify at your first test—maybe not even your second, or seventh. You may, but chances are, something will go amiss. Just look upon it as a chance to get to try again. Ask the advice of other participants, and try to make some contacts that may help as training partners. Don't sweat it; the worst thing that can happen is, you go home without a ribbon but with a dependable hunting partner, great companion, and memories of an enjoyable day in the field.

Finally, if it seems like all these tests and titles are a little too artificial or demanding, take some time off to remind yourself what it's all about. Crunch across iced ground and see the breath billow from your excited Golden. Sure, ribbons and titles are nice, but can it get any better than this moment of solitude out of doors with your best partner?

# Chapter Eleven

# When Gold Dogs Do Bad Things

Even good dogs, with good owners, do bad things sometimes. The real test of a good owner is how you deal with these situations. Until recently, even the best owners had little choice of where to turn for advice for dog behavior problems. Well-meaning but misguided training advice from friends, breeders, or even veterinarians or dog trainers without a scientific background in dog behavior too often only made things worse. Great strides have been made in recent years in canine behavioral therapy. Qualified behaviorists will consider both behavioral and medical therapies. As a first step in any serious behavior problem, a thorough veterinary examination should be performed.

Proper socialization, with exposure to many people, animals, and situations (including being left alone), along with obedience training, will go a long way toward the prevention of behavior problems. Like people, dogs are individuals, and some-

*Even the most golden of beings can sometimes do the darkest of deeds.*

times, with even the best guidance, they don't act like the angels we envisioned.

## Behavior Changes

Unprecedented behavior of any kind, but particularly persistent circling or pacing, disorientation, loss of balance, head pressing, hiding, tremors, seizures, lack of bowel or urine control, or dramatic change in appetite, is usually a sign of a physical problem and needs to be checked by your veterinarian.

The most common behavioral sign of disease is lethargy. A lethargic dog tends to show little interest in its surroundings. Possible causes could include:
• Infection—check for fever.
• Pain—check limbs, neck, and vertebrae for signs of discomfort upon movement; check mouth, ears, and eyes for signs of pain; check abdomen for pain; pain in the abdomen often causes dogs to stand in a hunched position.
• Sudden loss of vision.

- Poisoning—check gum color, pupil reaction; look for vomiting or signs of abdominal pain.
- Cancer.
- Metabolic diseases.

# Unruly Behavior

Goldens are large, active dogs, which is one of their major attractions. Unfortunately, it is one of the reasons they are most often put up for adoption. Many families find that, as much as they love their Goldens, they can't cope with their activity level, jumping, and barking.

---

*G O L D   N U G G E T*

### The Golden Rules

- *You get what you ask for.* Dogs repeat actions that bring them rewards, whether you intend for them to or not.
- *Mean what you say.* Lapses in consistency are ultimately unfair to the dog.
- *Say what you mean.* Your Golden takes his commands literally.
- *Train in the present.* Dogs live in the present, and they can only assume any punishment or reward is for their behavior at that time.
- *Punish yourself, not your dog.* Harsh or repeated punishment doesn't work. If punishment doesn't work the first time, why would it work the second, third, or fourth time?

---

## Hyperactivity

Hyperactivity is best dealt with by selecting a breed that fits your lifestyle. Goldens were initially developed for their ability to spend a long, strenuous day retrieving without tiring out. This means that throwing a ball for ten minutes is not going to tire your Golden. Goldens are energetic, intelligent dogs. If your dog is driving you crazy, it's probably because he's going crazy, through lack of stimulation. The best cure for an overactive Golden is lots of mental and physical exercise—a good run or swim, a fast-paced game, or a challenging obedience lesson. Also, a dog agility course is a great mind and body exerciser.

### Jumping Up

Jumping up to greet you is normal canine behavior, but it can be an irritating or dangerous one. Teach your dog to sit and stay so that you can kneel down to his level for greetings. When he does jump up, simply say *"No"* and step backward, so that his paws meet only air. Teaching your dog a special command that lets him know it's OK to jump up can actually help him know the difference.

Shutting your dog in another room when guests arrive will only make him more crazed to greet people, and ultimately worsen the problem. The more people he gets a chance to greet politely, the less excited he'll be about meeting new people, and the less inclined to jump on them. Have your guests kneel and greet your sitting Golden, then

*Most bad behaviors come from failure to communicate, rather than deliberate disobedience.*

send him to his special spot in the room where he can be part of the group without going crazy.

## Barking

You may think silence is golden, but your Golden may disagree. If your dog won't stop barking when you tell him to, distract him with a loud noise of your own. Begin to anticipate when your dog will start barking, distract him, and reward him for quiet behavior. You will actually create a better watchdog by discouraging your dog from barking at nonthreatening objects and encouraging him to bark at suspicious people. Allow your Golden to bark

momentarily at strangers, and then call him to you and praise him for quiet behavior, distracting him with an obedience exercise if need be.

A dog stuck in a pen in the backyard will bark. What else is there to do? Isolated dogs will often bark through frustration or as a means of getting attention and alleviating loneliness. Even if the attention gained includes punishment, they continue to bark in order to obtain the temporary presence of the owner.

The simplest solution is to move the dog's quarters to a less isolated location. Let the dog in your house, or fence in your entire yard. If barking occurs when you put your dog to

GOLD ★ STAR

Ollie was found wandering the streets, abandoned and in bad shape. Even after his physical problems were cured, serious behavioral problems remained. Ollie was so undersocialized and insecure that he barked nonstop, to the point that debarking or euthanasia seemed the only choices. Through the combined efforts of a behaviorist, obedience classes (for socialization only), citronella and shock collars, and an immeasurable amount of love and patience, Ollie learned to control himself, grew confident, and even earned his Canine Good Citizen and Therapy Dogs International certificates. Now Ollie teaches children to work through their fears, and shares the trust and love that he had finally found. He even found a new name: Jay-O-Bee's Lord Oliver Twist, CGC, TDI.

bed, move his bed into your bedroom, or condition him by rewarding him for successively longer periods of quiet behavior. The distraction of a special chew toy, given only at bedtime, may help alleviate barking. Remember, a sleeping dog can't bark, so exercise can be a big help. The dog that must spend the day home alone is a greater challenge. Again, the simplest solution is to change the situation, perhaps by adding another animal—a good excuse to get two dogs.

For stubborn barkers, a citronella collar is sometimes effective. These collars spray a squirt of citronella, which dogs don't like, whenever the dog barks. They are more effective and safer than bark-activated shock collars.

## Escaping

Golden Retrievers are smart dogs, sometimes too smart for their own good. Some apply their intelligence to finding escape routes from the yard. In most cases, their owners have helped to make them that way. They have helped their dog learn how to escape by making it easy at first, and then gradually trying to see if the minimal fix will work. Take the example of the new Golden owner and the old fence. The new owner surveys the fence and decides it might be tall enough and strong enough. When the dog demonstrates it was not tall enough, the owner tries to fix it by adding an extension to make it a bit taller. The problem is that the dog has learned that fences can be beaten, and will likely test the new fence. If the dog can jump that one, too, or dig under it, the owner is in for a problem; adding to the fence bit by bit is just the way you would teach a dog to jump Olympic heights. So don't use the same technique to teach your dog *not* to jump. If you want your dog to stay in the yard, make your yard escape-proof from the very beginning.

# Home Destruction

One of the golden moments of Golden ownership is the dog's joyful greeting upon your return home. That moment will be tarnished if you open your door to the sight of home vandalism. The vandal is your loving dog, telling you how much he loves you as only a dog can do.

**Boredom:** But before we get to how your dog destroying your home is a token of his love for you, let's talk about the ones in which it isn't. Puppies are natural demolition dogs, and they vandalize for the sheer ecstasy that only a search-and-destroy mission can provide. The best cure, besides adulthood, is supervision and prevention. Adult Goldens still may destroy items through frustration or boredom. The best way to deal with these dogs is to tire them with both physical and mental exercise an hour or so before leaving them. Several toys are available that can provide hours of entertainment; for example, some can be filled with peanut butter or treats in such a way that it takes the dog a very long time to extract the food from the toy.

**Anxiety:** Often, adult dogs continue to vandalize your home, but the cause is seldom boredom and they won't just outgrow it. The Golden Retriever is an extremely devoted dog, and its owners tend to be equally devoted. They chose a Golden Retriever in part because of the breed's desire to be close to its family. The problem for many Goldens arises when their people leave them all alone. Being left alone is an extremely stressful situation for these highly social animals and they react by becoming agitated and trying to escape from confinement. Perhaps they reason that if they can just get out of the house, they will be reunited with their people. The telltale signature of a dog suffering from this *separation anxiety* is that most of their destructive behavior is focused around doors and windows. Some owners believe the dog is "spiting" them, and they punish the dog. Unfortunately, punishment is ineffective because it actually increases the anxiety level of the dog, that comes to both look forward to and dread the owner's return.

Separation anxiety should be treated like any other fear, that is, working up gradually. This is done by leaving the dog alone for very short periods of time and gradually working to longer periods, taking care never to allow the dog to become

---

*G O L D   N U G G E T*

### Oral Fixations

Goldens need things to carry around, and if you don't provide them, they will find them among your precious items. A durable hard rubber toy is ideal for unsupervised times, but a soft fleece toy is even more cherished. Never give small balls, socks, or anything that could be chewed up or swallowed—they can kill.

---

*Goldens are very social, and being left alone can be very stressful for them.*

anxious during any session. When you *must* leave your dog for long periods during the conditioning program, leave him in a different part of the house than the one in which the conditioning sessions take place. Thus, you won't undo all of your work if he becomes overly stressed by your long absence.

When you return home, no matter what the condition of the house or how much you missed your dog, greet him calmly. Then have him perform a simple trick or obedience exercise so that you have an excuse to praise him. In severe cases, your veterinarian can prescribe antianxiety medications to help your pet deal with being left alone. It takes a lot of patience, and often a great deal of self-control, but it's not fair to you or your dog to let this situation continue. It will only get worse.

> ## GOLD NUGGET
>
> ### Severe Separation Anxiety
> New drug therapy for separation anxiety is available from your veterinarian. It is best used as part of a training program, not a permanent crutch.

## Fearfulness

Even the most stable of Golden Retrievers can sometimes develop illogical fears, or phobias. The most common are fears of strange people or dogs, and gunshots or thunder.

Every once in a while, a particularly imaginative Golden will come up with a bizarre fear all his own, but the fear can usually be treated using the same general concepts.

The cardinal rule of working with a fearful dog is to never push him into situations that might overwhelm him. Some people erroneously think the best way to deal with a scared dog is to inundate him with the very thing he's afraid of until he gets used to it. This concept (called *flooding*) doesn't work, because the dog is usually so terrified he never gets over his fear enough to realize the situation is safe.

Never coddle your Golden when he acts afraid, because it reinforces the behavior. It's always useful if your Golden knows a few simple commands; as we have said, performing these exercises correctly gives you a reason to praise your dog and also increases his sense of security because he knows what's expected of him.

In some cases, the dog is petrified at even the lowest level of exposure to whatever he is scared of. If that happens, you may have to use antianxiety drugs in conjunction with training to calm your dog enough to make progress. This is when you need the advice of a behaviorist.

## Strangers

Golden Retrievers are characteristically gregarious with strangers; however, an occasional dog will be wary of those it doesn't know. Shy dogs are like shy people in some

ways: They are not so much afraid of people as they are of being the center of attention of people. Unfortunately, the most common advice given to cure shyness in dogs is to have a lot of strange people pay attention to the dog. This usually does little except scare the dog further. Never force a dog that is afraid of people to be petted by somebody he doesn't know. Strangers should be asked to ignore shy dogs, even when approached by the dog. When the dog gets braver, have the stranger offer him a tidbit, at first while not even looking at the dog.

## Noises

Most Goldens with hunting experience get excited at the sound of a gunshot, associating it with the chance to retrieve. Some, however, are gun shy. Although a startle reaction is normal, gun-shy dogs will run away, hide, pant, and shake. Fear of thunder or gunshots is a common problem in older dogs. To see a normally happy-go-lucky Golden Retriever quivering and panting in the closet at the slight rumblings of a distant thunderstorm is a sad sight, and it only gets worse with time. It is also dangerous, as some dogs have been lost by running blindly away, an all too common tragedy during Fourth of July celebrations. The time to do something about it is at the first sign of trouble. Try to avoid fostering these fears. Act cheerful when a thunderstorm strikes, and play with your dog or give him a tidbit. Once a dog develops a noise phobia, try to find a recording of that noise. Play it at a very low level and reward him for calm behavior. Gradually increase the intensity and duration of the recording.

**Note:** A program of gradual desensitization, with the dog exposed to the frightening person or thing and then rewarded for calm behavior, is time-consuming but the best way to alleviate any fear.

# Loss of Housebreaking

A physical examination is warranted any time a formerly housebroken dog begins to soil the house. You and your veterinarian will need to consider the following possibilities:

• Older dogs may simply not have the bladder control they had as youngsters; a doggy door is the best solution.

• Older spayed females may dribble urine, especially when sleeping; ask your veterinarian about drug therapies.

• Frequent urination of small amounts—especially if the urine is bloody or dark—may indicate an infection of the urinary tract. Such infections must be treated promptly. Consult your veterinarian.

• Increased urine production can be a sign of kidney disease or diabetes, which your veterinarian can test for and treat. Never restrict water from these dogs; a doggy door is a better way to cope.

• Sometimes, a housebroken dog will be forced to soil the house because of a bout of diarrhea, and afterwards will continue to soil in the same area. If this happens, restrict

*Most Goldens want to be good; your job is to help them find the way.*

that area from the dog, deodorize the area with an enzymatic cleaner from a pet supply store, and revert to basic housebreaking lessons originally taught as a puppy.

• Male dogs may lift their leg inside of the house as a means of marking it as theirs. Castration will often solve this problem as long as it is performed before the habit has become established; otherwise, diligent deodorizing and the use of some dog-deterring odorants, available at pet stores, may help.

• Submissive dogs, especially young females, may urinate upon greeting you; punishment only makes this submissive urination worse. For these dogs, be careful not to bend over or otherwise dominate them, and keep your greetings calm. Submissive urination is usually outgrown as the dog gains more confidence.

• Some dogs defecate or urinate due to the stress of separation anxiety; you must treat the anxiety to cure the symptom. Dogs that mess their cage when left in it are usually suffering from separation anxiety or anxiety about being closed in a cage. Other telltale signs of anxiety-produced elimination are drooling, scratching, and escape-oriented behavior. You need to treat separation anxiety and start cage training again, placing the dog in it for a short period of time and working up gradually to longer times. Dogs that suffer from cage claustrophobia but not separation anxiety do better if left loose in a dog-proofed room or yard.

# Aggression

It's hard to believe an amiable Golden, friend to all, could ever be aggressive. True, aggressive behavior is very uncommon, even rare, in Goldens. Nonetheless, the Golden Retriever is a large dog, and like all dogs, can sometimes act in ways that make us uncomfortable. Many types of aggression can occur in dogs, and the treatment for them can be very different. Some new dog owners have difficulty telling if their dog is actually behaving aggressively.

### Is It Really Aggression?

Puppies and dogs play by growling and biting. Usually, they play with their littermates this way, but if yours is an only puppy, you will just have to do. You need to know the difference between true aggression and playful aggression. Look for these clues that tell you it's all in good fun:

• Wagging tail
• Down on elbows in front, with the rump in the air (the play-bow)
• Barks intermingled with growls
• Lying down or rolling over

## Sudden Aggression
Aggressive behavior is usually not a sign of disease unless it is totally unprecedented. It can be a sign of pain, an endocrine problem, or a brain problem. Such dogs should be seen by a neurologist or a veterinarian specializing in behavior.

- Bounding leaps or running in circles
- Mouthing or chewing on you or other objects

On the other hand, look for these clues to know you'd better watch out:
- Low growl combined with a direct stare
- Tail held stiffly
- Sudden, unpredictable bites
- Growling or biting in defense of food, toys, or bed
- Growling or biting in response to punishment

Chances are your Golden is simply playing. Still, this doesn't mean you should let him use you as a chewstick. When your pup bites you, simply say *"Ouch! No!"* and remove your hand (or other part) from his mouth. Replace it with a toy. Hitting your dog is uncalled for; he was just trying to play and meant no harm. Hitting also is a form of aggression that could give your dog the idea that he had better try (bite) harder next time because you're playing the game a lot rougher. You don't want to encourage playful aggression, but you don't want to punish it. You want to redirect it.

## Aggression Toward Other Dogs

If your dog is really acting aggressively rather than playfully, you need to decide if the aggression is directed toward other dogs and animals or toward people. Aggression toward other animals does not mean a dog will be aggressive toward people.

*Most Goldens get along well with other animals, but much depends upon how they were raised and introduced to them.*

Many dogs are aggressive toward strange dogs but friendly toward housemates, and many dogs chase small animals such as cats.

Aggression toward strange dogs is a biologically normal trait of canines, but one that is not suitable for dogs in today's world. It is natural for your dog to defend his territory against strange dogs. The problem develops when you try to introduce a new dog into the home, or when your dog thinks the world is his personal territory. Most Goldens get along well together, but some are more territorial than others, and some dogs, like some people, just don't see eye to eye.

**Housemates:** Problems between housemates are mostly likely to occur between dogs of the same sex and same age. Seniority counts for a lot in the dog world, and a young pup will usually grow up respecting its elders. Sometimes, a youngster gets aspirations to be top dog, however, or two dogs of about the same age never quite decided which one was leadership material. Then the trouble starts. Remember to decide first if this is natural rough play behavior between the two. An occasional disagreement, too, is normal. A disagreement that draws blood or leaves one dog screaming, or in which the two dogs cannot be separated is a potential problem. Repeated disagreements spell trouble. Neutering one or both males in a two male dominance battle can sometimes help, but neutering females will not.

It's human nature to soothe the underdog and punish the bully, but you'd be doing the underdog the worst favor you could. If your dogs are fighting for dominance, they are doing so in part because, in the dog world, the dominant dog gets the lion's share of the most precious resources. You, and your attention, are the very most precious resource your dog can have. If you now give your attention to the loser, the winner will only try harder to beat the daylights out of the loser so your attention will go where it should go—to the winner. You will do your losing dog the best favor if you treat the winning dog like a king, and the losing dog like a prince. This means you always greet, pet, and feed the top dog first. It goes against human nature, but it goes *with* dog nature.

### Aggression Toward Humans

Much has been made of dominance problems in dogs; they probably occur less often than is thought, but when they do occur, the results can be aggression toward family members. Aggression toward humans is uncommon (but not unheard of) in Goldens. When it does happen, the best advice is to seek advice from a dog behaviorist (not a dog trainer!) or a veterinarian with special training in behavior. Remember, dominance aggression does not refer to the occasional nip in play or even disobedience. It is a serious situation in which the dog actively challenges and bites, or threatens to bite, a member of the family.

*Tug games are fine for most Goldens, but for those dogs in which dominance or aggression may be a problem these games should be stopped.*

Because it is a serious situation, it calls for serious treatment that is not called for in other cases.

Dominance aggression most often occurs as a result of competition over a resource—such as trying to remove food or a toy, encroaching on the dog's sleeping quarters, or trying to step past him in a narrow hall—or during a perceived display of dominance by the owner, such as petting, grooming, scolding, or leading. Dogs may act more aggressively toward family members than toward strangers, and treat the family members in a dominant way, such as walking stiffly, staring, standing over them, and ignoring commands. Punishment usually only elicits further aggression.

Dominance aggression is more common in males than females, and occasionally (but not always) castration can help. Your veterinarian can give your intact (unneutered) male dog a drug that will temporarily cause its hormonal state to be that of a neutered dog as a test to see if castration might help. Spaying a female will not help, and may even hinder, curing dominance aggression.

Owners of such dogs inevitably feel guilty, and wonder, "Where did I go wrong?" The fault is not entirely theirs. Although some actions of the owner may have helped create the problem, these same actions would not have produced dominance aggression in dogs that were not already predisposed to the problem. In predisposed dogs, owners who act in ways to foster the dog's opinion of himself as king can add to the problem. What would convince a dog that he ranked over a person? Actions such as:

- Petting the dog on demand
- Feeding the dog before eating your own meal
- Allowing the dog to go first through doorways
- Allowing the dog to win at games
- Allowing the dog to have his way when he acts aggressively
- Fearing the dog
- Not punishing the dog for initial instances of aggression

**Treatment:** Treatment consists of putting the dog in his place, without direct confrontations. A popular training method from several years ago was the "alpha roll," in which you roll the dominant dog over on his back into a submissive position. However, this is a good way to get bitten and most canine behaviorists now think it is a bad idea.

It's best to avoid situations that might lead to a showdown. If your dog only growls, however, and *never* bites, you may be able to nip the behavior in the bud before you get nipped yourself by scolding or physically correcting the dog. If your dog is likely to bite, but you still want to try, talk to your veterinarian about temporary drug therapy to calm him sufficiently during initial training, and consider having your dog wear a muzzle.

When dealing with a dominant-aggressive dog, you must cease and desist any of your behaviors that tell the dog he is the boss. As much pleasure as you may get from petting your dog absentmindedly as you watch TV, you can't. There will be no more free lunches, and no more free pets, for your dog. From now on, your dog must work for his petting, his praise, and even his food. The work will be simple—just obeying simple commands from you. He must sit when you tell him to sit, and wait until you have gone through doorways first. When he thrusts his head into your lap to be petted, you must ignore him. When you want to pet him, you must first have him obey some simple commands, and then pet him sparingly as a reward. Yes, it's tough love, but it may be your problem dog's only chance. Please note, that such tough love is not necessary for most Goldens—only those with serious dominance-aggression problems.

As with people, dogs can develop an astounding array of behavioral problems. Nobody, and no dog, is perfect. Our dogs seldom act and do exactly as we would wish them to; neither do our friends and family. We try to change what we can, gripe about the rest, and love them regardless.

# Chapter Twelve

# Breeding 24-Karat Gold

One of the most unfortunate aspects of owning dogs is that so many people feel the compulsion to breed them. The reasons always seem good at the time, and it is a tempting idea. The problem lies, however, in the fates of the resulting puppies.

## Please Don't Litter

Consider this: In 1998 the AKC registered 18,785 Golden Retriever litters, along with 65,681 individuals. As wonderful and popular as Goldens are, it's difficult to believe that 65,681 good new homes were waiting for these puppies.

What happens to them? Some die of natural causes, but far more die of unnatural causes; of these, most are struck by cars, and some are poisoned, shot, or die of neglect. Of the survivors, many are lost or given away, and then given away by their next owners, and so on. Some end up in the dog pound or in rescue. Some go to puppy mills or backyard

*A healthy, quality puppy is no accident.*

breeders where they are bred as often as possible until they cease to produce and are dumped or euthanized. Some are tied to a chain or stuck in a pen in the backyard where they will sit without companionship, activity, or shelter for the next ten years. Some are physically abused. Some do find good homes, mostly with people who cared enough to do their homework and find good, responsible breeders. In other words, if you want to attract good buyers, you need to be a good breeder. Can you live up the requirements of a good breeder (page 25)? Do the potential parents of your litter live up to the requirements of good breeding stock (page 170)? Remember:
• Unless your Golden has proven herself by earning titles and awards in competitions, or by being an outstanding working dog, you may have a difficult time finding good buyers.
• The average litter size for Goldens is eight puppies. Breeding so you can keep one pup ignores the fact that seven others may not get a good home—or may be ransacking your home for the next ten years.

• Selling puppies will not come close to reimbursing you for the health clearances, stud fee, prenatal care, whelping complications, possible Caesarian section, supplemental feeding, puppy food, vaccinations, advertising, and a staggering investment of time and energy.

---

*G O L D   N U G G E T*

### Spaying and Neutering

Most veterinarians advocate neutering and spaying dogs that will not be used for breeding. Not only do these procedures negate the chance of accidental litters, but they also do away with the headaches of dealing with a dog in season. In addition, some health benefits are associated with these procedures.

Spaying (surgical removal of ovaries and uterus) before the first season drastically reduces the chances of breast or uterine cancer. Castration (surgical removal of the testicles) virtually eliminates the chance of testicular cancer. The health benefits are somewhat offset, however, by the lowered metabolism in spayed females, resulting in slight weight gain unless the dog is fed a somewhat lower amount of food. Spayed females also have a higher incidence of urinary incontinence, hypothyroidism, and hemangiosarcoma. Neutered males have similar changes, but to a lesser degree.

---

• Responsible breeders have spent years researching genetics and the breed, breed only the best specimens, and screen for hereditary defects in order to obtain superior puppies. Unless you have done the same, you are doing yourself, your dog, the puppies, any buyers, and the breed a great disservice.

# Genetic Considerations

If you're contemplating breeding, it's assumed you've educated yourself about your dog's strengths and weaknesses, have had the appropriate health clearances (page 79), and are familiar with Golden Retriever lines and studs. Choosing a stud will involve several considerations:

**1.** You want an overall nice dog. This dog should have earned titles and awards, which not only give an impartial evaluation of him, but will also be helpful in finding good homes.

**2.** You want the dog to complement your bitch, so that the two do not share the same faults.

**3.** You want the dog to come from a consistently good background.

**4.** You want to find an older dog that has already proven he can live to a healthy old age.

**5.** You want to avoid using a very popular sire. Every dog has recessive deleterious genes, even the nicest and most popular studs. It is far better for the health of the breed to maintain genetic diversity by breeding to an equally nice, but less used, stud.

**6.** In most cases, you should avoid breeding to a dog closely related to your bitch.

You should calculate how inbred the resulting puppies would be. The coefficient of inbreeding (COI) refers to the probability that a dog will have identical copies of the same gene that both trace back to the same ancestor. For example, the COI of pups from a sibling to sibling or parent to offspring mating is 25 percent; the COI from a mating of a half–brother to half–sister is 12.5 percent. You can calculate this by hand or with some computer pedigree programs.

### G O L D   N U G G E T

**The Gene Pool Is a Puddle**
The fact that Goldens all descend from a limited number of founders, and that 99 percent of Goldens can trace to four breedings, signifies that Goldens as a breed are already considerably inbred. This is true of a number of breeds.

Because many deleterious genes are recessive (meaning it takes two identical copies for them to exert their effects on the individual), it's generally a good idea to avoid breedings with high COIs. As a general rule, dogs that are less closely related are more likely to produce healthy and long-lived offspring.

*Finding the perfect match to be the parents of the next generation takes lots of study, searching, and good luck.*

*The best puppies come from the best parents with the best breeders.*

Whereas dogs with high COIs are the results of inbreeding, low COIs result from outcrossing. Many geneticists now advocate breeding for the lowest possible COI; however, some compromises will likely need to be made in order to find a dog that otherwise fits your criteria.

GOLD ★ STAR

One of the most amazing producers of any breed and all time is Ch Amberac's Asterling Aruba, the dam of 32 Champions, including four BIS winners, and grandam to the all-time top-winning BIS winner and all-time top-winning National specialty winner. Perhaps it's no wonder: She was herself the first Golden to be owner-handled to BIS and SDHF, proving quality begets quality.

GOLD NUGGET

**Polygenic Traits**
Although much attention has been paid to dominant and recessive traits, most traits of interest to dog breeders are polygenic traits, that is, traits that are controlled by the influences of many gene pairs, and thus may not be expressed in an all-or-none fashion. The depth of the golden coat coloration is one such trait; height is another.

# Breeding and Whelping

### Breeding

Arrangements should be made with the stud owner well in advance of the breeding. A written contract should spell out what expenses you'll be responsible for and what will happen if no puppies are born. Count the days from the first sign of estrus carefully, but don't rely on them to determine the right day to breed. If you're shipping your bitch or there's a lot riding on this breeding, consider monitoring her estrous cycle by means of ovulation timing. Vaginal smears can also give some guidance, but are not nearly as reliable. An experienced stud dog is usually the most reliable indicator of the right time to breed. Most people breed the pair on alternate days for two to three breedings. Dogs ovu-

*G O L D    N U G G E T*

**Pyometra**

If a mucous discharge from the vulva is accompanied by lethargy and fever, contact your veterinarian immediately. It could be a sign of pyometra, a potentially fatal uterine infection that most commonly appears in the month or two after estrus. The best treatment is spaying, but medical drug therapy is sometimes successful for valuable breeding bitches.

late all their eggs within 48 hours, so the idea that runts result from eggs fertilized from later breedings is not valid.

### Pregnancy

Dog gestation is 63 days. Around day 18 to 21, implantation occurs, and during this time some pregnant

*Every Golden carries a small sample of the breed's gene pool.*

dogs will appear nauseated and even vomit. Human pregnancy tests don't work because, unlike in humans, even unbred bitches have the same rise in "pregnancy" hormones as pregnant ones do. This is why dogs have pseudopregnancies; it's normal dog physiology because hormonally, they are the same as dogs with real pregnancies. However, a new dog pregnancy test (Repro CHEK) can detect the presence of relaxin, a substance produced by the placenta of a pregnant dog after implantation, typically by days 21 to 25 post-fertilization.

## G O L D   N U G G E T

### Calculating Inbreeding

One way to measure inbreeding is by a technique called path analysis.

**1.** Redraw your dog's pedigree, but instead of writing it out in the traditional manner, every time the same name appears on *both* the sire's side and the dam's side, write the name only once.

**2.** Draw a path from your dog's sire, back through each of its ancestors to that common ancestor.

**3.** Do the same through your dog's dam. Now you should have a circular path through several generations that goes via both the sire's and dam's sides of your dog's pedigree.

**4.** Count the number of steps in the circular pathway from your dog to the common ancestor, and subtract 1 from that number.

**5.** The contribution of each step in the pathway is $(\frac{1}{2})^n$, where $n$ is the number you got in step 4. For example, $(\frac{1}{2})^2$ is 0.25, $(\frac{1}{2})^3$ is 0.125, and $(\frac{1}{2})^4$ is 0.0625.

**6.** Many dogs will have more than one ancestor common to both sire and dam, so repeat these steps for each common ancestor.

**7.** Add the contributions of each path together, for example, $(\frac{1}{2})^3 + (\frac{1}{2})^4 + (\frac{1}{2})^6$ to obtain the F value, also called the coefficient of inbreeding (COI). In this example F = 0.125 + 0.0625 + 0.015625 = 0.203125, or in plain language, a COI of about 20 percent.

**8.** Note that the COI tends to increase the more generations you include in your analysis, so it's more proper to refer to it as a "COI of an X generation pedigree," where X is the number of generation you included.

**9.** COI also increases if the common ancestor is itself inbred. The adjustment to the calculation is made by multiplying the $(\frac{1}{2})^n$ result by $(1 + F^a)$, where $F^a$ is the COI of the common ancestor. So, if the common ancestor had a COI of 0.0125, then you would multiply the $(\frac{1}{2})^n$ value by 1.0125.

*Good puppies grow into great adults—with lots of help from great breeders and owners.*

By about day 35, pregnancy can be determined with ultrasound. Other signs that often develop by then are a mucous discharge from the vagina and enlarged pinkish nipples. In the last week of pregnancy, radiographs can be used to count fetal skeletons. The knowledge of how many puppies to expect can be useful for knowing when the bitch has finished whelping.

GOLD ★ STAR

Ch Misty Morn's Sunset is the breeds' top-producing sire, fathering 127 Champion offspring.

GOLD NUGGET

**Pink Pigment**
Don't be alarmed that the pups all have pink noses and feet; the darker pigment takes several days, and even weeks, to develop.

## Whelping

Begin taking the expectant mother's temperature morning and evening every day starting about a week before the due date. When her temperature drops dramatically, to around 98°F (37°C) and stays there, you can anticipate pups within the next 12 hours. She will become increasingly restless and uncomfortable; eventually, she will begin to strain with contractions. Each puppy is preceded by a water bag; once this has burst, the puppy should be born soon. If a puppy appears stuck, you can use a washcloth and gently pull it downward along with the mother's contractions; however, never pull a puppy by a limb, tail, or its head. You may wish to help the mother clear the pup's face so it can breathe, and you may wish to tie off the umbilical cord. Do this by tying dental floss around the cord about ¾ of an inch (around 2 cm) from the pup, and then cutting the cord on the side away from the pup. Make sure that for every pup that comes out, a placenta comes out, too. Allow the dam to eat one placenta if she wants to, as they contain important hormones, but they contribute to diarrhea and one is enough.

## Neonates

Monitor the puppies to make sure they are getting milk; pups with cleft palates will have milk bubbling out of their nostrils as they nurse. Use a baby scale to make sure the puppies gain weight every day. Puppies can't regulate their body temperature, and chilling can kill them. Never feed a chilled puppy. Place the pups in a warm box when the dam must leave. Maintain the temperature in at least one part of the whelping box at about 85°F (29°C) for the first week, 80°F (27°C) for the second week, and 75°F (24°C) for the third and fourth weeks. Overheating and dehydration can have just as devastating effects. Make sure the pups can crawl away from the heat.

Some neonates die for no apparent reason; canine herpes claims some young pups. Affected pups cry piteously and will not nurse. The herpes virus cannot replicate in high temperatures, and some pups have

---

### GOLD NUGGET

## You may have a whelping emergency if:

- More than 24 hours have passed since her temperature dropped without the onset of contractions.
- More than two hours of intermittent contractions have passed without progressing to hard, forceful contractions.
- More than 30 minutes of strong contractions have passed without producing a puppy.
- More than 15 minutes have passed since part of a puppy protruded through the vulva and the puppy makes no progress.
- Large amounts of blood are passed during whelping.

been saved by placing them in incubators at the first sign of symptoms. If you suspect canine herpes, keep your pups very warm and consult your veterinarian immediately.

The puppies' eyes will begin to open at around 10 days of age, and the ears at around two weeks. Around this time, they will also start attempting to walk. Be sure to give them solid footing—not slippery newspaper.

The dam will begin to wean them at around four to six weeks. Introduce them to pureed puppy food just before they nurse, and be prepared to clean up a major disaster area. You should be checking the dam's mammary glands throughout for signs of mastitis, which include pain, bloody discharge, and hard swelling. Home care includes hot compresses and gentle expression of the affected gland, while preventing pups from nursing from it. Call your veterinarian for advice; antibiotics may be necessary.

# Deworming

Ask your veterinarian about the vaccination and deworming regimen he or she recommends. Some controversy exists about the traditional series of shots and deworming, so your veterinarian may give you choices and you should be ready to ask questions.

## Intestinal Parasites

Even pups from the most fastidious breeders get worms. This is because some types of larval worms

---

**GOLD NUGGET**

**Dewclaws**

If you are going to remove dewclaws (see page 73), you need to do so around three days of age.

become encysted in the dam's body long before she ever became pregnant, perhaps when she herself was a pup. Here they lie dormant and immune from worming until hormonal changes caused by her pregnancy activate them, and then they infect her fetuses or her newborns through her milk.

**Ascarids:** The ascarid *Toxocara canis* is found in most pups. Toxocaris can be spread to people as well as dogs through infested feces. Infected puppies can also become quite ill, with heavy infestations leading to convulsions or death. Symptoms include a rough coat, potbelly, and wasting muscles. Sometimes, adult worms can be seen in vomit or feces. Puppies should be wormed at least twice for Toxocaris, and many protocols advocate more frequent worming.

**Hookworms:** Hookworms are especially prevalent in warm, humid climates. Puppies with heavy infestations have bloody, black, or tarry diarrhea, and can become anemic and die. Adult dogs usually build up an immunity to hookworms, although some dogs have chronic hookworm disease.

**Whipworms:** Whipworms inhabit the large intestine; heavy infestation

GOLD NUGGET

## When to Worm

Dogs should not be routinely wormed unless a fecal test has demonstrated they actually have worms. Over-the-counter wormers are largely ineffective and less safe than those available through your veterinarian. Most deworming regimens require repeated doses several weeks apart to be effective. Some heartworm preventives also prevent most types of intestinal worms, but not tapeworms. The number one prevention for most worms is daily removal of feces from the yard.

can cause diarrhea, anemia, and weight loss. Unlike some other types of internal parasites, dogs do not develop an immunity to whipworms. Treatment consists of repeated deworming, often every other month for a year.

**Protozoan intestinal parasites:** Puppies and dogs also suffer from protozoan intestinal parasites, such as coccidia and giardia.

Coccidia are often associated with diarrhea, but many infected dogs show no apparent symptoms; therefore, the importance of coccidial infection in dogs is not well understood at present. A stool sample is needed for diagnosis. Affected dogs respond well to supportive treatment and drugs to do away with the coccidia.

Giardia are found fairly commonly in puppies and dogs. An infection can cause chronic or intermittent diarrhea, but may also have no symptoms. Giardiasis can be diagnosed with a stool sample, and is more likely to be found in loose or light-colored stool. Giardiasis can be treated with drug therapy.

# Vaccinations

Vaccinations save lives. Although some disagreement exists over whether too many vaccinations can have detrimental effects on some dogs, the fact that they are absolutely essential to your dog's well-being is beyond dispute.

Puppy vaccinations are some of the most vital, but most confusing, of all the vaccinations your dog will receive. Puppies receive their dam's immunity from colostrum, the special type of milk the dam produces in the first days of life. This is why it is important that the dam is properly immunized long before breeding, and that her pups are able to nurse from her. The immunity gained from the dam will wear off after several weeks; then the pup will be susceptible to disease unless you provide immunity through vaccinations. The problem is that there is no way to know exactly when this passive immunity will wear off, and vaccinations given before that time are ineffective. Therefore, you must revaccinate over a period of weeks so that your pup will not be unprotected and will receive effective immunity. That's why puppies get a series of shots instead of just one or two.

Vaccinations are available for several diseases. Some vaccinations are mandatory from a legal standpoint, some mandatory from a good sense standpoint, and some optional. Recent studies have implicated repeated vaccinations with combinations of vaccines with some autoimmune problems (see page 79). Some veterinarians therefore recommend staggering different types of vaccines, and discourage overvaccination. They also discourage vaccination of any dog that is under stress or not feeling well. Many dogs seem to feel under the weather for a day or so after getting their vaccinations, so don't schedule your appointment the day before boarding, a trip, or a big doggy event.

The common vaccines are:

**Rabies:** Rabies is passed mostly through the saliva of carnivores and bats. It is inevitably fatal once symptoms have appeared. Because of its deadly consequences, state laws mandate that all dogs must be vaccinated. The initial rabies vaccination should be given at around three to four months of age, again one year from the first vaccination, and then every three years, although to comply with local law you may have to give a booster every year.

**Distemper:** Distemper is seen almost exclusively in unvaccinated puppies. Initial symptoms are upper-respiratory problems and fever, followed by vomiting, diarrhea, and neurologic signs. Very young

*Drinking natural water is fun, but it can expose dogs to giardia or other toxins.*

puppies—about six weeks old— usually get a distemper/measles vaccination, because the measles fraction can give temporary immunity even in the presence of maternal antibodies. Subsequent distemper inoculations are given every three to four weeks until the pup is about sixteen weeks old.

**Hepatitis:** Infectious canine hepatitis type 1 is most often seen in puppies. It is highly contagious and incurable, even fatal. An adenovirus, called CAV-1, is the causative agent, but vaccination is with CAV-2, which works just as well but doesn't result in the "blue-eye" reaction that CAV-1 caused when it was used years ago.

**Leptospirosis:** Leptospirosis is a bacterial disease, more prevalent in rural areas. It causes serious liver, kidney, and blood abnormalities. Vaccination for "lepto" does not protect against all strains of leptospirosis, and even then only protects for about three to six months. A small percentage of puppies have a transient adverse reaction to the vaccination; therefore, some people prefer not to include lepto in their vaccination regimen.

**Parvovirus:** Parvo is extremely contagious, often fatal, and can remain in the environment for years. Its effects are especially devastating in puppies. Vaccination for parvovirus is often interfered with by maternal antibodies; for this reason, three vaccinations by the age of 16 weeks are recommended, with an optional fourth at around 18 to 20 weeks.

**Coronavirus:** Coronavirus causes extreme diarrhea when accompanied with parvovirus, in rare cases results in death. Younger dogs are most adversely affected. A vaccination is available, but is considered optional currently.

**Tracheobronchitis (kennel cough):** Kennel cough is highly contagious. Vaccinations are available, but the problem is that kennel cough can be caused by many different infectious agents. The vaccines protect against the most common ones (CPIV, CAV-2, and Bordetella), but not all. Their effects also do not last very long. For these reasons, and because kennel cough is not fatal, some people prefer not to vaccinate for it.

**Lyme disease:** Lyme disease is known to cause severe problems in humans, but its effects in dogs are less clear-cut. A vaccination is available but is not universally accepted as necessary. Only dogs living in endemic areas should be considered candidates for Lyme disease vaccination.

Several respected veterinary teaching hospitals have recently revised their vaccination protocols to include fewer booster shots. One such protocol suggests giving a three-shot series for puppies, each shot containing parvovirus, adenovirus 2 (CAV-2), parainfluenza (CPIV), and distemper, with one rabies vaccination at 16 weeks. Following this, a booster is given one year later, and then subsequent boosters are given every three years.

*The breeder's job doesn't stop when the pups are weaned. Each pup must be socialized and introduced to the big world ahead.*

Other respected epidemiologists disagree and prefer the traditional vaccination schedule. Confer with your veterinarian about current thinking on the matter. One thing is certain: No matter what their possible side effects, vaccinations are a good thing, and all dogs must be vaccinated for their health as well as the health of others.

## The World Ahead

It's important that the puppies get out to meet people and be socialized in the ways of the world, but at the same time you must be careful about contagious diseases. Your pups should be leash-trained and crate-trained before they go to new homes. They should have spent time away from their littermates. They should have had some car riding experience and met men, women, and children. During all this, they've probably burrowed deep into your heart.

Now comes the hardest part of breeding a litter: saying good-bye to the pups you've grown to love, and whose futures you are sealing with your choices about potential buyers. Screen carefully, and don't be afraid to ask prying questions. Your puppies are depending on you.

Of course, you could always keep them all...

# Chapter Thirteen

# The Golden Years

If you're fortunate, one day you'll look at your youngster and realize his face has silvered and gait has stiffened. Athough in typical Golden fashion, he may still be a puppy at heart, you have to realize you are now blessed with a Golden oldie.

All dogs age at different rates, but by nine years of age, most Golden Retrievers can be considered in their golden years. The average lifespan for a Golden is about 10 to 13 years, although rare individuals have lived to 19 years of age. You may have depended on your dog for years when he was younger, now it is your turn to let your dog lean on you.

## Care of the Older Golden

**Exercise:** Many people have this macho idea that their dog will never slow down with age, and many Goldens feed this perception with their playful attitudes. Dogs do age at different rates, but staying in a state of denial about your dog's increasing age or decreasing abili-

*For many people, the golden years are most golden of all.*

ties is not doing him any favors. It's important to keep your older dog relatively active, without putting too much stress on his joints. If your dog is sore the next day, you have probably asked too much. Swimming is an excellent low-impact exercise.

While Goldens of any age enjoy a soft, warm bed, it is an absolute necessity for an older Golden. Arthritis is a common cause of intermittent stiffness and lameness, and it can be helped with heat, a soft bed, moderate exercise, and possibly drug therapy. New arthritis medications have made a huge difference in the quality of life for many older dogs, but not every dog can use them. Ask your veterinarian to evaluate your dog.

**Feeding:** Both physical activity and metabolic rates decrease in older animals, so they require fewer calories to maintain the same weight. Obesity stresses the dog's system and joints; however, very old dogs often tend to lose weight, which can be equally bad. Your dog needs a little bit of fat so that he has something to fall back on if he gets sick. High-quality (not quantity) protein is especially important for older

*Goldens in the winter of their lives can still enjoy the outdoors, but special care should be taken for their well-being.*

Some older dogs become cranky and impatient, especially when dealing with puppies or boisterous children, but don't just excuse behavioral changes, especially if sudden, as due simply to aging. They could be symptoms of pain or disease.

**Sensory loss:** Older dogs may experience hearing or visual loss. Dogs that have been subjected to a lot of gunfire during their hunting days may have accelerated hearing loss. Dogs with hearing loss can learn hand gestures and also respond to vibrations.

Dogs with gradual vision loss can cope well as long as they are kept in familiar surroundings, and extra safety precautions are followed. For

dogs. Most older dogs do not require a special diet unless they have a particular medical need for it.

Older dogs should be fed several small meals instead of one large meal, and should be fed on time. Moistening dry food or feeding canned food can help a dog with dental problems enjoy his meal. He may enjoy eating while lying down or eating from a raised platform.

**Behavior:** Older dogs tend to like a simpler life, and although they still are up for adventure, that adventure may need to be toned down or abbreviated. Long trips can be grueling for an older dog, and boarding in a kennel may be upsetting. Consider getting a house-sitter your dog knows if you want to go on vacation.

GOLD STAR

Many Goldens have remained active well into their golden years. Housemates Kyrie Genever, Am Can UDTX and Anthea of Setherwood Am Can UDTX both earned their TDX titles at age 10; Ch Kyrie Jaen Cobi UD earned her Utility title at age 11; Ch Lorelei's Golden Robber finished his championship at age 12; Am Can Ch Heron Acres Sandcastle Am Can UDTX *** WCX MH, UKC HRCH & UD, NAHRA MHR WR, OD was still earning titles at age 12, and several hunters have still been active retrieving ducks well into their teens.

*Many Goldens have remained active hunting companions after their first decade, but such dogs are the result of a lifetime of good care, combined with good genes and good fortune.*

example, block open stairways or pools, don't move furniture, and place sound or scent beacons throughout the house or yard to help the dog locate specific landmarks. Also lay pathways, such as gravel, or block walkways outdoors, and carpet runners indoors. The slight haziness that appears in the older dog's pupils is normal and has minimal effect upon vision, but some dogs, especially those with diabetes, may develop cataracts. These can be seen as almost white through the dog's pupils. The lens can be removed by a veterinary ophthalmologist if the cataract is severe.

GOLD ★ STAR

Proving that you can teach an old dog new tricks, Christmas Holly AX, OAJ, VMAD, VS, VJ didn't start in agility until she was eight years old. She made up for lost time by winning over 200 ribbons and titles in all venues of agility, was ranked in the top 10 agility Goldens at age 10, and at 11½ years of age, Holly became the oldest Golden to earn the AKC Agility Excellent title—and with nearly all perfect scores!

# Health of the Older Golden

The older Golden should have a checkup at least twice a year. Blood tests can detect early stages of treatable diseases. Although older dogs present a somewhat greater anesthesia risk, this can be largely negated by first screening with a complete medical workup.

• The immune system may be less effective in older dogs, so it is increasingly important to shield your dog from infectious disease, chilling, overheating, and any stressful conditions. At the same time, an older dog that is never exposed to other dogs may not need to be vaccinated as often or for as many diseases as a younger dog. This is an area of current controversy, and you should discuss this with your veterinarian.

*Even when wild games and days in the field are faded memories, the older Golden still has much to relish in life.*

• Vomiting and diarrhea in an old dog can signal many different problems; keep in mind that an older dog cannot tolerate the dehydration that results from continued vomiting or diarrhea, and you should not let it continue unchecked.

• Like people, dogs lose skin moisture as they age, and though dogs don't have to worry about wrinkles, their skin can become dry and itchy. Regular brushing can help by stimulating oil production.

• Older dogs tend to have a stronger body odor, but don't just ignore increased odors. They could indicate specific problems, such as periodontal disease, impacted anal sacs, seborrhea, ear infections, or even kidney disease. In general, any ailment that an older dog has is magnified in severity compared to the same problems in a younger dog.

**Cushing's syndrome (hyperadrenocorticism)** is seen mostly in older dogs, and is characterized by increased drinking and urination, a potbellied appearance, symmetrical hair loss on the body, darkened skin, and susceptibility to infections. Diagnosis is with a blood test. Treatment is with drug therapy.

If you are lucky enough to have a Golden oldie, you still must accept that your time together is all the more precious and ultimately will end. Heart disease, kidney failure, and cancer eventually claim most of these senior citizens. Early detection can help delay their effects, but, unfortunately, can seldom prevent them ultimately.

# When You've Done Everything

Despite the best of care, a time will come when neither you nor your veterinarian can prevent your dear friend from succumbing to old age or an incurable illness. It seems hard to believe that you will have to say good-bye to such a wonderful companion, family member, and partner in adventure. That dogs live such a short time compared to humans is a cruel fact, but one that you must ultimately face.

Many terminal illnesses make your dog feel very ill, and there comes a point where your desire to keep your friend with you as long as possible may not be the kindest thing for either of you. If your dog consistently declines to eat, this is usually a sign that she doesn't feel well, and a signal that you must begin to face the prospect of doing what is best for your beloved friend.

Euthanasia is a difficult and personal decision that no one wants to make. Consider whether your dog has a reasonable chance of getting better, and how she seems to feel. Ask yourself if your dog is getting pleasure out of life, and if she enjoys most of her days. Financial considerations can be a factor if it means going into debt in exchange for just a little while longer. Your own emotional state must also be considered. For every person the ultimate point is different. Most people probably put off doing something for longer than is really the kindest thing to do, because they don't want to act in haste and be haunted by thoughts that just maybe it was a temporary setback. And of course, they put it off because they can't stand the thought.

We all wish that if our dog has to go, she would fall asleep and never

---

*GOLD NUGGET*

## Symptoms and their possible causes in older dogs:

- Diarrhea: kidney or liver disease, pancreatitis, colitis.
- Coughing: heart disease, tracheal collapse, lung cancer, pneumonia.
- Difficulty eating: periodontal disease, oral tumors.
- Decreased appetite: kidney, liver, or heart disease, pancreatitis, cancer.
- Increased appetite: diabetes, Cushing's syndrome.
- Weight loss: heart, liver or kidney disease, diabetes, cancer.
- Abdominal distention: heart or kidney disease, Cushing's syndrome, tumor.
- Increased urination: diabetes, kidney or liver disease, cystitis, Cushing's syndrome.
- Limping: arthritis, hip or elbow dysplasia, degenerative myelopathy.
- Nasal discharge: tumor, periodontal disease, nasal foreign body.

GOLD NUGGET

**Pet Loss**
Rainbow Bridge Tribute Page
dealing with the loss of a pet:
http://rainbowbridge.tierranet.
com/bridge.htm

wake up. This, unfortunately, seldom happens. Even when it does, you are left with the regret that you never got to say good-bye. The closest you can come to this is with euthanasia. Euthanasia is painless and involves giving an overdose of an anesthetic. Essentially, the dog will fall asleep and never wake up.

*The friend of a lifetime...we wish these days could last forever.*

Note that a dog with very poor circulation may do so gradually, but the process is still painless.

If you do decide that euthanasia is the kindest farewell gesture for your beloved pet, discuss with your veterinarian beforehand what will happen. You may ask about giving your dog a tranquilizer beforehand, or having the doctor meet you at home. Although it won't be easy, try to remain with your dog so that her last moments will be filled with your love. Try to recall the wonderful times you have shared and realize that however painful losing such a once-in-a-lifetime friend is, it is better than never having had such a partner at all.

# Eternally in Your Heart

Many people who regarded their Golden Retriever as a member of the family nonetheless feel embarrassed at the grief they feel at her loss. Yet this dog has often functioned as a surrogate child, best friend, and confidant. Partnership with a pet can be one of the closest and most stable relationships in many people's lives. Unfortunately, the support from friends that comes with human loss is too often absent with pet loss. Such well-meaning but ill-informed statements as "he was just a dog" or "just get another one" do little to ease the pain, but the truth is that many people simply don't know how to react and probably aren't really as callous as they might sound. Many people share and understand your feelings, however, and pet bereavement counselors are available at many veterinary schools.

After losing such a cherished friend, many people say they will never get another dog. True, no dog will ever take the place of your dog, but another Golden can be a welcome diversion that can help keep you from dwelling on the loss of your first pet. True also, by getting another dog you are sentencing yourself to the same grief in another ten years or so, but wouldn't you rather have that than miss out on a second once-in-a-lifetime dog?

The loss of a companion may mark the end of an era for you, a time when you and your Golden

## GOLD NUGGET

### Life Expectancy
Many people feel Goldens aren't living as long as they used to, whether from the cumulative effects of inbreeding with a limited gene pool or environmental toxins. No data exist, but in either case it should be noted that many people have unrealistic expectations about life expectancy for their dog, based upon the publicity given to unusually long-lived individuals.

grew up or grew old together—truly the end of a Golden age. Perhaps the best tribute is to open your heart to another Golden, and your future to another Golden Age.

*Remember the happy times...*

# Useful Addresses and Literature

## Organizations

Agility Association of Canada (AAC)
RR#2, Lucan, Ontario N0N 2J0
Tel: (519) 657-7636

American Dog Owner's Association
1654 Columbia Turnpike
Castleton, NY 12033
Tel: (518) 477-8469
e-mail: adoa@global2000.net

American Kennel Club (AKC)
5580 Centerview Drive
Raleigh, NC 27606-3390
Tel: (919) 233-9767
e-mail: info@akc.org
http://www.akc.org/

American Temperament Testing
  Society
P.O. Box 397, Fenton, MO 63026
Tel: (314) 225-5346
http://www.atts.org/

Canine Eye Registration Foundation
  (CERF)
1248 Lynn Hall, Purdue University
West Lafayette, IN 47907
Tel: (765) 494-8179
http://www.vet.purdue.edu:80/
  ~yshen/cerf.html

Canadian Kennel Club
89 Skyway Avenue
Suite 100
Etobicoke, Ontario
M9W 6R4
Tel: (800) 250-8040
e-mail: information@ckc.ca
http://www.ckc.ca/

Canine Performance Events
  (CPE)
P.O. Box 445
Walled Lake, MI 48390
e-mail: cpe-agility@juno.com

Golden Retriever Club of America
  (GRCA)
C/O Secretary, P.O. Box 932
Bonner, MT 59823
National Information Line:
  (281) 861-0820
http://www.grca.org/

GRCA Breeder Contact
Anne McGuire
Tel: (281) 861-0820
http://www.grca.org/puppy.htm

GRCA National Rescue Hotline
Tel: (281) 861-0820
http://www.grca.org/rescue.htm

Hunting Retriever Club
100 East Kilgore Road
Kalamazoo, MI 49002-5584
http://www.hrc-ukc.com/

National Retriever Club of Canada
http://www.cadvision.com/murrayt/
nrcc.html

National Retrieving Club
5 Deblyn Lane
West Chester, PA 19382
Tel: (610) 793-2402
http://www.working-retriever.com/
nrc/

North American Dog Agility Council
(NADAC)
HCR 2, Box 277
St. Maries, ID 83861
Tel: (208) 689-3803
e-mail: nelsonk9@iea.com

North American Hunting Retriever
Association (NAHRA)
P.O. Box 5159
Fredericksburg, VA 22403
Tel: (540) 286-0625
e-mail: nahra@juno.com
http://www.nahra.org/

Orthopedic Foundation for Animals
2300 E. Nifong Blvd.
Columbia, MO 65201
Tel: (573) 442-0418
e-mail: ofa@offa.org
http://www.offa.org/

PennHlp
Synbiotics Corporation
11011 Via Frontera
San Diego, CA 92127
Tel: (800) 228-4305
http://www.vet.upenn.edu/pennhip/
index.html

Therapy Dogs International
88 Bartley Road
Flanders, NJ 07836
Tel: (973) 252-9800
e-mail tdi@gti.net
http://www.tdi-dog.org/

United Kennel Club (UKC)
100 East Kilgore Road
Kalamazoo, MI 49001-5593
Tel: (616) 343-9020
http://www.ukcdogs.com/

United States Dog Agility
Association (USDAA)
P.O. Box 850995
Richardson, TX 75085-0955
Tel: (972) 231-9700
e-mail: info@usdaa.com
http://www.usdaa.com/

## Periodicals

*AKC Afield* (covers AKC field activities of many breeds) and *AKC Gazette* (covers general aspects of all breeds)

AKC Order Desk
5580 Centerview Drive
Raleigh, NC 27606-3390
Tel: (919) 233-9767
e-mail: orderdesk@akc.org
http://www.akc.org/insideAKC/
  resources/subs.cfm

*Bird Dog and Retriever News*
563 17th Avenue NW
New Brighton, MN 55112
Tel: (651) 636-8045
e-mail: publisher@wwwBird-Dog-
  News.com
http://www.bird-dog-news.com/

*Clean Run* (covers agility)
35 Walnut Street
Turners Falls, MA 01376
Tel: (800) 311-6503
Fax: (413) 863-8303
e-mail: info@cleanrun.com
http://www.cleanrun.com/

*Dog World Magazine*
500 N. Dearborn, Suite 1100
Chicago, IL 60610
Tel: (312) 396-0600
e-mail: info@dogworldmag.com

*Front and Finish* (covers obedience)
H & S Publications, Inc.
P.O. Box 333
Galesburg, IL 61402-0333
e-mail: frntfnsh@galesburg.net
http://www.frontfinish.com/

Golden Retriever Club of America
  Yearbooks
Order through the GRCA
P.O. Box 69
Berthoud, CO 80513
http://www.grca.org/sales.htm

*The Golden Retriever News*
Available only to members of the
  GRCA
http://www.grca.org/grnews.htm
Note: *Best of the Golden Retriever News*, available to nonmembers; order through the GRCA
P.O. Box 69
Berthoud, CO 80513
http://www.grca.org/sales.htm

*The Golden Retriever Review*
Chris Carpenter
Simi Valley, CA 93065
e-mail: caceac@earthlink.net
http://www.grreview.com/

*Gun Dog*
(covers field activities of gun dogs)
P.O. Box 343
Mt. Morris, IL 61054
http://www.stovpub.com/gundog/

*NAHRA News*
P.O. Box 5159
Fredericksburg, VA 22403
Tel: (540) 286-0625
e-mail: nahra@juno.com

*The Retriever Journal*
Tel: (800) 447-7367
e-mail: webmaster@villagepress.
  com
http://www.villagepress.com/
  wildwood/rj2.html

*Retrievers Online* (covers field trial and hunting retrievers)
1457 Heights Rd., R.R. # 3
Lindsay, Ontario K9V 4R3
Canada
Tel: (705) 793-3556
http://starsouth.com/online/

## Books

Bauer, Nona Kilgore. *The World of the Golden Retriever: Dog For All Seasons.* Neptune City, NJ: TFH, 1993.

Cairns, Julie. *The Golden Retriever; An Owner's Guide To A Happy, Healthy Pet.* New York: Howell Book House, 1995.

Coile, D. Caroline. *Encyclopedia of Dog Breeds.* Hauppauge, NY: Barron's Educational Series, 1998.

———. *Show Me! A Dog Showing Primer.* Hauppauge, NY: Barron's Educational Series, 1997.

Dobbs, Jim; Phyllis Dobbs and Alice Woodyard. *Tri-Tronics Retriever Training.* Tucson, AZ: Tri-Tronics, Inc. (P.O. Box 17660, Tucson, AZ, 85731; (800) 456-4343), 1993.

Fischer, Gertrude. *The New Complete Golden Retriever.* New York: Howell Book House, 1984.

Foss, Valerie. *Golden Retrievers Today.* New York: Howell Book House, 1994.

———. *The Ultimate Golden Retriever.* New York: IDG, 1997.

Milner, Robert. *Retriever Training for the Duck Hunter.* Huntington Beach, CA: Safari Press, 1996.

Mueller, Larry. *Speed Train Your Own Retriever : The Quick, Efficient, Proven System for Training a Finished Dog.* Mechanicsburg, PA: Stackpole Books, 1987.

Nicholas, Anna Katherine. *Book of the Golden Retriever.* Neptune City, NJ: TFH, 1983.

Quinn, Tom. *The Working Retrievers.* New York: Lyons Press, 1998.

Robinson, Jerome. *Training the Hunting Retriever.* New York: Lyons Press, 1999.

Rutherford, Clarice and Cherylon Loveland. *Retriever Puppy Training; The Right Start for Hunting.* Loveland, CO: Alpine, 1988.

Schlehr, Marcia. *The New Golden Retriever.* New York: Howell Book House, 1996.

Spencer, James B. *Retriever Training Tests.* Loveland, CO: Alpine, 1997.

———. *Training Retrievers for Marshes and Meadows.* Loveland, CO: Alpine, 1998.

Strombeck, Donald. *Home-prepared Dog and Cat Diets: The Healthful Alternative.* Ames, IA: Iowa State University Press, 1999.

Sucher, Jaime. *Golden Retrievers: Everything About Purchase, Care, Nutrition, Diseases, Behavior, and Breeding.* Hauppauge, NY: Barron's Educational Series, 1996.

Tarrant, Bill. *Hey Pup, Fetch It Up!: The Complete Retriever Training Book.* Mechanicsburg, PA: Stackpole Books, 1993.

## Videos

AKC Golden Retriever Standard
Video WT107
AKC Order Desk
5580 Centerview Drive
Raleigh, NC 27606-3390
Tel: (919) 233-9767
e-mail: orderdesk@akc.org
http://www.akc.org/insideAKC/resources/vidbreed.cfm
For a list of other videos available from the AKC: http://www.akc.org/insideAKC/resources/vidgi.cfm and http://www.akc.org/insideAKC/resources/vidshevt.cfm

The Golden Retriever by Rachel Page Elliott for the GRCA
Order through the GRCA
P.O. Box 69
Berthoud, CO 80513
http://www.grca.org/sales.htm

Grooming Your Golden
Delaware Valley Golden Retriever Rescue
Attn: Video Order, P.O. Box 2321
Sinking Springs, PA 19608-0321
http://www.dvgrr.org/goodies.html

Hunting Tests for Retrievers
Video WT107
AKC Order Desk
5580 Centerview Drive
Raleigh, NC 27606-3390
Tel: (919) 233-9767
e-mail: orderdesk@akc.org

Total Retriever Training and Marking Videos by Mike Lardy
Younglove Broadcast Services, Inc.
P.O. Box 79
Metamora, MI 48455
Tel: (800) 848-5963
http://starsouth.com/lardy/
http://starsouth.com/lardy/trtwml.htm

## Web Pages

| | |
|---|---|
| Animal CPR | http://members.aol.com/henryhbk/acpr.html |
| Bird Dog and Retriever News | http://www.bird-dog-news.com/ |
| The Dog Agility Page | http://www.dogpatch.org/agility/ |
| The Dog Obedience and Training Page | http://www.dogpatch.org/obed/ |
| Dr. P's Dog Training Links | http://www.uwsp.edu/acad/psych/dog/dog.htm |
| Field and Hunting Retriever | http://huntingretriever.com/fieldhuntingretriever. htm |
| Goldens Afield | http://www.goldensafield.com/ |
| Golden Links | http://camlok.com/GoldenLinks.html |
| Golden Retrievers in Cyberspace | http://www.golden-retriever.com/ |
| Golden Retriever Review Website | http://www.grreview.com/ |
| Goldens at Work | http://www.goldensatwork.com/ |
| Hunting Retriever Judge's Corner | http://scribers.midwest.net/timg/ |
| Infodog Dog Show Site | http://www.infodog.com/main.htm |
| National Animal Poison Control Center | http://www.napcc.aspca.org/ |
| Tel: (800) 548-2423 | |
| Operant Conditioning in Dog Training | http://mmg2.im.med.umich.edu/~kleung/ training.html |
| Rainbow Bridge Tribute Page | http://rainbowbridge.tierranet.com/bridge.htm |
| Rescue Information Center | http://labrynth.simplenet.com/ric/ |
| Retriever Hall of Fame | http://starsouth.com/hallfame/ |
| Retriever Field Trial Home Page | http://www.working-retriever.com/retriever-trials/ |
| Steppin' Up-Date Obedience Site | http://www.dogpro.com/terriarnold/newsletter/ Newsletter1.htm |
| Take a BowWow Training Site | http://www.takeabowwow.com/ |
| The Tracking Page | http://personal.cfw.com/~dtratnac/ |
| Versatile Dogs | http://www.versatiledogs.com/ |
| The Working Goldens | http://www.working-retriever.com/ working-goldens/ |
| Working Retriever Central | http://www.working-retriever.com/ |

# Index